Praise for the Poetry of Luis J. Rodríguez

Poems Across the Pavement

"Luis Rodríguez dives into the human heart & conveys those small hard-to-describe glimpses of the human spirit in transition & change. He exhumes from the human experiences what we try to forget & offers it to the reader, still breathing & alive & meaningful. His voice is on the verge of the world, a day break."
—Jimmy Santiago Baca

The Concrete River

The Concrete River "is inspiring for its emotional import and intellect. Rodríguez is an exciting young Chicano poet who promises to be a major voice in the landscape of American poetry."—Tino Villanueva, *Boston Review*

"Rodríguez writes from the inside out, with great knowledge, passion, and compassion...Highly recommended for contemporary poetry and multicultural collections."—*Library Journal*

"This poetry is of the barrio yet stubbornly refuses to be confined in it—Rodríguez' perceptive gaze and storyteller's gift transport his world across neighborhood boundaries."—*Publishers Weekly*

"What makes Luis Rodríguez' poetry attractive is not its raw honesty but rather the lyrical beauty that suddenly emerges at unpredictable moments. There are lines that bloom like the flowers he is always making reference to."—*The American Poetry Review*

"This is poetry at its most powerful and uncompromising: poetry which cannot fail to move."—*British Bulletin of Publications on Latin America, The Caribbean, Portugal and Spain*

"Luis J. Rodríguez, an important new voice, writes of the barrio, the steel mills and street gangs...In his bag of tools, his words, Rodríguez knows just which to use to chisel well-sculpted poetry. His is the gift of sharing."—*The Indianapolis News*

"The poems in this volume have a brutal yet shimmering intensity that registers the poignant humor and pathos of many Chicanos' lives."—*American Book Review*

Trochemoche

"While filled with the heart and words of Chicano culture, Rodríguez's poems transcend the scope of race and ethnicity. The topics he addresses in this book—relationships, justice, love, and the irony of daily life—are, or should be, the subjects that envelop us all. It is this universality, cloaked in the specific encounters of his life, that makes his writing as gripping to readers living in inner-city America as to those living in small-town USA. The context of Rodríguez's poetry may be urbane, but his subject matter is as much about what's on the inside as what's on the outside."
　　—Aaron McCarroll Gallegos, *Sojourners*

"Fifty-one poems of elegance, image and grace."
　　—*New City* (Chicago)

"In fusing childhood experience of working life, love and family with current labors and lusts,...these poems make clear their voracity."—*Publishers Weekly*

"...poetic discourses drenched in autobiography and rooted in reality, poignant testimonies that reflect the often brutal starkness of the contemporary Hispanic experience."—*Library Journal*

"In the vernacular of the barrio and the street, this poet writes hard-hitting, bitter poems with flashes of wry self-mockery. Rodríguez's poems offer a mature reader both pleasure and insights."—*VOYA*

"The voices of *Trochemoche* are truly unforgettable."
　　—*World Literature Today*

"In the cadence of struggle, of street talk, and the salient speech of the social outcast, Rodríguez is raw, honest, passionate, and lyrical."—*Multicultural Perspectives*

My Nature Is Hunger:
New & Selected Poems
1989-2004

by
Luis J. Rodríguez

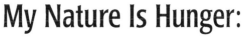

A Curbstone Press / Rattle Edition

Printed in Canada on acid-free paper by Best Book/Transcontinental
Cover design: Stone Graphics
Cover artwork: oil painting by Mark Vallen

NATIONAL
ENDOWMENT
FOR THE ARTS

This book was published with the support
of the Connecticut Commission on Culture
and Tourism, Frieda C. Fox Foundation,
National Endowment for the Arts, and
donations from many individuals.
We are very grateful for this support.

Connecticut Commission
on Culture & Tourism

Library of Congress Cataloging-in-Publication Data

Rodriguez, Luis J., 1954-
  My nature is hunger : new & selected poems, 1989-2004 / by Luis J.
Rodriguez.— 1st ed.
    p. cm.
  ISBN-13: 978-1-931896-24-5 (pbk. : acid-free paper)
  ISBN-10: 1-931896-24-0
  1. Mexican Americans—Poetry. I. Title.
  PS3568.O34879M9 2005
  811'.54—dc22   2005017726

A CURBSTONE / RATTLE EDITION
funded by the Frieda C. Fox Foundation

CURBSTONE PRESS   321 Jackson Street   Willimantic, CT 06226
phone: 860-423-5110   e-mail: info@curbstone.org
http://www.curbstone.org

ACKNOWLEDGMENTS:

Thanks to the following publications and venues where the new poems first appeared:

"My Nature Is Hunger" in *Power Lines: A Decade of Poetry from Chicago's Guild Complex,*" edited by Julia Parson-Nesbitt, Luis J. Rodríguez & Michael Warr (Chicago: Tia Chucha Press, 1999), *Other Voices Anthology* (online); *Blackmailpress 7* (online).

"Mickey Mouse Pancakes" in *Rattle* Magazine, Fall 1999, Los Angeles; *Other Voices Anthology* (online).

"The Cockroaches I Married" and other poems read on the air, WBEZ-FM, Chicago "848" Program; *Other Voices Anthology* (online).

"My Name's Not Rodríguez" in *The Progressive* magazine; *Bum Rush the Page: A Def Poetry Jam,* edited by Tony Medina and Louise Reyes Rivera (NYC: Three Rivers Press, 2001); *Cantos Al Sexto Sol: An Anthology of Aztlanahuac Writings,* edited by Roberto Rodriguez, Patrisia Gonzalez and Cecilio Garcia Camarillo (San Antonio: Wings Press, 2002); *Other Voices Anthology*; *Blackmailpress 7, K-Code: The Real Italian Lifestyle & Culture Magazine.*

"¡Sí, Se Puede! Yes, We Can!" in the children's book *¡Sí, Se Puede! Yes, We Can!* written by Diane Cohn, illustrated by Francisco Delgado (El Paso, TX: Cinco Puntos Press, 2002).

"Passersby" in *Other Voices Anthology.*

"Exiled in the Country of Reason" in *Other Voices Anthology*; *Blackmailpress 7.*

"Poems to Ponder in Times of War and Uncertainty" in *Poets Against the War* (online); *Long Shot Magazine*; *Logos: A Journal of Modern Society & Culture* (online).

"Someday a Man Will Come" in the *People's Tribune/Tribuno del Pueblo.*

The selected poems appeared in the following books:

Poems across the Pavement (Chicago: Tia Chucha Press, 1989);
The Concrete River (Willimantic, CT: Curbstone Press, 1991);
Trochemoche (Willimantic, CT: Curbstone Press, 1998)

New and selected poems appeared in the following recordings: *My Name's Not Rodriguez* by Luis J. Rodríguez and Seven Rabbit, spoken word/music CD for Dos Manos Records (Los Angeles, 2002); *Live at Beyond Baroque 2* with Luis J. Rodríguez, Viggo Mortensen, Marvin Bell, Patricia Smith, Saul Williams, Regie Gibson, Mike McGee, Georganne Deen, Mark Eleveld (LA: two-disc CD, Perceval Press/EM Press, Fall 2004); *From the Earth to the Sky: Music and Spoken Word to Benefit Tia Chucha's Centro Cultural* (L.A., Dos Manos Records, 2004); *Una Domanda Alla Risposta* (A Question for an Answer) with Flycat for V.S.O.P/Skill to Deal Records (Milan, Italy, 1998); *Poetics of Peace: Vital Voices in Troubled Times* with Alice Walker, Luis Rodríguez, Michael Meade, Jack Kornfield & Orland Bishop (Mosaic Audio, Seattle, WA, 2002); *Snake in the Heart: Poems and Music by Chicago Spoken Word Performers* for Tia Chucha Press (Chicago, 1994); *In Their Own Voices: A Century of Recorded Poetry* for Rhino Records/Word Beat, 1996; and *The Poetry Box* (L.A., Shout! Factory, 2005).

Thanks to the numerous books, magazines, anthologies, and other publications where these poems have also appeared, including *The Outlaw Bible of American Poetry*, edited by Alan Kaufman (New York City: Thunder's Mouth Press, 1999); *From Totems to Hip-Hop: A Multicultural Anthology of Poetry Across the Americas, 1900-2002*, edited by Ishmael Reed (NYC: Thunder's Mouth Press, 2003); *The Spoken Word Revolution (Slam, Hip Hop & the Poetry of a New Generation)*, edited by Mark Eleveld (Naperville, IL: Sourcebooks, 2003); *Poets One: Anthology of World Poetry Festival in Heidelberg, Germany, 2003*, and others.

Thanks to the US Embassy in Berlin, Germany for publishing a special edition chapbook of new poems, *My Nature is Hunger*, for the Re-Writing America: Multi-Ethnic Perspectives in Literature and the Media, Blaubeuren, Germany, November 2004. A special thanks to Sher Zabaszkiewicz and Matt Cohen for creating hand-made art books and broadsides for the new poems, including the limited-numbered *Seven* and *Dos Mujeres* art books, with translations by Jorge Cabrera and Trini Rodriguez.

And my humble gratitude to the Lila Wallace-Reader's Digest Fund, the Lannan Foundation, the Hispanic Heritage Foundation, the Illinois Arts Council, the Illinois Association of Teachers of English, the Chicago Department of Cultural Affairs, the North Carolina Arts Council, the California Arts Council, the National Association for Poetry Therapy, the Wisdom in Action Foundation, the Border Book Festival, PEN Oakland, Chicago Artists Abroad, PEN International's "Next Generation" selection during the 54th World Congress in Montreal and Toronto, the Poetry Center of San Francisco State University, among others, for fellowships, residencies and awards during the writing of many of these poems.

For a single poem to be born
we must kill things
many, many things we love
— Ryuichi Tamura

CONTENTS

from Poems Across the Pavement – 1989

from The Concrete River – 1991

from Trochemoche – 1998

New Poems

from
Poems Across the Pavement – 1989

Running to America

For Alfonso and Maria Estela Rodríguez, migrants

They are night shadows violating borders,
fingers curled through chain-link fences,
hiding from infra-red eyes, dodging 30-30 bullets.
They leave familiar smells, warmth and sounds
as ancient as the trampled stones.

Running to America.

There is a woman in her finest border-crossing wear:
A purple blouse from an older sister,
a pair of worn shoes from a church bazaar,
a tattered coat from a former lover.

There is a child dressed in black,
fear sparkling from dark Indian eyes,
clinging to a headless Barbie doll.

And the men, some hardened, quiet,
others young and loud—you see something
like this in prisons. Soon they will cross
on their bellies, kissing black earth,

then run to America.

Strange voices whisper behind garbage cans,
beneath freeway passes, next to broken bottles.
The spatter of words, textured and multi-colored,
invoke demons.

They must run to America.

Their skin, color of earth, is a brand
for all the great ranchers, for the killing floors
on Soto Street and as slaughter
for the garment row. Still they come:
A hungry people have no country.

Their tears are the grease of the bobbing machines
that rip into cloth
that make clothes
that keep you warm.

They have endured the sun's stranglehold,
el cortito, foundry heats and dark caves
of mines, swallowing men.

Still they come, wandering bravely
through the thickness of this strange land's
maddening ambivalence.

Their cries are singed with fires of hope.
Their babies are born with a lion
in their hearts.

Who can confine them?
Who can tell them
which lines never to cross?

For the green rivers, for their looted gold,
escaping the blood of a land
that threatens to drown them,
they have come,

running to America.

Somebody Was Breaking Windows

Somebody was breaking the windows
out of a 1970s Ford.
Somebody's anger, for who knows what,
shattered the fragile mirror of sleep,
the morning silence
and chatter of birds.
A sledge hammer in both hands then crashed
onto the side of the car,
down on the hood,
through the front grill and headlights.
This Humboldt Park street screamed
in the rage of a single young man.
Nobody got out of their homes.
Nobody did anything.
The dude kept yelling
and tearing into the car.
Nobody claimed it.
I looked out of the window as he swung again.
Next to me was a woman.
We had just awakened after a night of lovemaking.
Her six-year-old daughter was asleep
on a rug in the living room.
The woman placed her arms around me
and we both watched through the louver blinds.
Pieces of the car tumbled
onto steamed asphalt.
Man hands to create it.
Man hands to destroy it.
Something about being so mad
and taking it out on a car.
Anybody's car.
I mean, cars get killed everyday.
I understood this pain.

And every time he swung down on the metal,
I felt the blue heat swim up his veins.
I sensed the seething eye staring from his chest,
the gleam of sweat on his neck,
the anger of a thousand sneers
—the storm of bright lights
into the abyss of an eyeball.
Lonely? Out of work? Out of time?
I knew this pain. I wanted to be there,
to yell out with him,
to squeeze out the violence
that gnawed at his throat.
I wanted to be the sledge hammer,
to be the crush of steel on glass,
to be this angry young man,
a woman at my side.

Rosalie has Candles

Rosalie has candles in a circle around her bed.
One night as I lay on a couch in a tequila stupor,
she takes off my shoes and trousers,
pulls a cover over me and snips two inches of hair
from my head. She places the hair in a glass
near the candles. I don't know why.
I don't know why she searches for me.
I don't know how she finds me in the bars.
I don't know why she ridicules the women I like
and uses me to meet men.
Rosalie usually finds solace in a glass
of whiskey. In my face she finds the same thing.
I don't know why. We argue too much.
We feign caring and then hurt each other
with indifference. With others we are tough
and mean. But in the quiet of darkness
we hold each other and caress like kittens.
She says she can only make love to someone
when she is drunk. She says she loves men
but has lesbian friends.
She loves being looked at. I want to hide.
She hates struggle. That's all I do.
She has Gods to pray to. I just curse.
I don't know what she sees in my face,
or hands for that matter. I only know
she needs me like whiskey.

The Monster

It erupted into our lives:
Two guys in jeans shoved it through the door
—heaving & grunting & biting lower lips.

A large industrial sewing machine.
We called it "the monster."

It came on a winter's day,
rented out of mother's pay.
Once in the living room
the walls seemed to cave in around it.

Black footsteps to our door
brought heaps of cloth for Mama to sew.
Noises of war burst out of the living room.
Rafters rattled. Floors farted
—the radio going into static
each time the needle ripped into fabric.

Many nights I'd get up from bed,
wander squinty-eyed down a hallway
and peer through a dust-covered blanket
to where Mama and the monster
did nightly battle.

I could see Mama through the yellow haze
of a single light bulb.
She slouched over the machine.
Her eyes almost closed.
Her hair in disheveled braids;

each stitch binding her life
to scraps of cloth.

Palmas

Palmas swayed on a rickety porch
near an old eaten-up tree
and plucked at a six-string:
The guitar man of the 'hood.

Fluid fingers moved across the neck
like a warm wind across one's brow.

Each chord filled with pain,
glory and boozed-up nights.

Every note sweating.

On Saturdays, Palmas jammed with local dudes.
They played in his honor on the nights
he didn't show up.

The guitar man—so sick, so tired,
but, man, he played so sweet.

I often wondered what gave Palmas his magic.
Blues bands wanted him.
Norteño bands wanted him.
Jazz musicians called out his name
from the bandstand.

He played Wes Montgomery
as if the dude were living inside his head.

He played crisp *corridos* and *Jarocho* blues
and seemed to make Jeff Beck
float through the living room window.

Yet he didn't venture too far beyond his rickety porch.

Sometimes he sat alone in his room,
the guitar on a corner of an unmade bed.

The last I heard, he played only
when the heroin in his body
gave him a booking.

Piece by Piece

Piece by piece
They tear at you:
Peeling away layers of being,
Lying about who you are,
Speaking for your dreams.

In the squalor of their eyes
You are an outlaw.
Dressing you in a jacket of lies
—tailor-made in steel—
You fit their perfect picture.

Take it off!
Make your own mantle.
Question the interrogators.
Eyeball the death in their gaze.
Say you won't succumb.
Say you won't believe them
When they rename you.
Say you won't accept their codes,
Their colors, their putrid morals.

Here you have a way.
Here you can sing victory.
Here you are not a conquered race
Perpetual victim
—the sullen face in a thunderstorm.

Hands/minds, they are carving out
A sanctuary. Use these weapons
Against them. Use your given gifts
—they are not stone.

The Calling

The calling came to me while I languished
in my room, while I whittled away my youth
in jail cells and damp barrio fields.

It brought me to life, out of captivity,
in a street-scarred and tattooed place
I called body.

Until then I waited silently,
a deafening clamor in my head,
but voiceless to all around,
hidden from America's eyes,
a brown boy without a name,

I would sing into a solitary
tape recorder, music never to be heard.
I would write my thoughts
in scrambled English;
I would take photos in my mind
—plan out new parks, bushy green, concrete free,
new places to play and think.

Waiting. Then it came. The calling.
It brought me out of my room.
It forced me to escape night captors
in street prisons.

It called me to war, to be writer,
to be scientist and march with the soldiers
of change.

It called me from the shadows, out of the wreckage
of my barrio—from among those
who did not exist.

I waited all of 16 years for this time.
Somehow, unexpected, I was called.

from
The Concrete River – 1991

Watts Bleeds

Watts bleeds, leaving stained reminders
on dusty sidewalks. Here where I strut alone,
as glass lays broken by my feet
and a blanket of darkness is slung
across the wood shacks of *nuestra colonia.*

Watts bleeds, dripping from carcasses of dreams.
Where despair is old people sitting on torn patio sofas
with empty eyes and children running down alleys
with big sticks.

Watts bleeds on vacant lots and burned-out building
—temples desolated by a people's rage.

Where fear is a deep river. Where hate is an overgrown weed.

Watts bleeds, even as we laugh, recall good times,
drink and welcome daylight through the broken windshield
of an old Impala.

Here is Watts of my youth, where teachers threw me
from classroom to classroom, not knowing where I could fit in.

Where I learned to fight or run, where I zigzagged down alleys,
jumped over fences, and raced by graffiti
on crumbling factory walls.

Where we played between the boxcars,
bleeding from the broken limbs and torn flesh,
and where years later we shot up heroin
in the playground of our childhood.

Watts bleeds as the shadow of the damned
engulfs all the *chinga* of our lives.

In the warmth of a summer night, gunshots echo their deadly song
through the silence of fear, prelude to a heartbeat.

Watts bleeds as I bled, getting laid-off from work,
standing by my baby's crib, touching his soft cheek
and fingering his small hand, as dreams shatter again,
dreams of fathers for little men.

Watts bleeds and the city hemorrhages,
unable to stop the flow from this swollen and festering sore.

Oh bloom, you trampled flower, come alive as once
you tried to do from the ashes.

Watts, bleeding and angry, you will be free.

Tía Chucha

Every few years Tía Chucha would visit the family
in a tornado of song and open us up
as if we were an overripe avocado.
She was a dumpy, black-haired
creature of upheaval who often came unannounced
with a bag of presents, including homemade
perfumes and colognes that smelled something like
rotting fish on a hot day at the tuna cannery.

They said she was crazy. Oh sure, she once ran out naked
to catch the postman with a letter that didn't belong to us.
I mean, she had this annoying habit of boarding city buses
and singing at the top of her voice—one bus driver
even refused to go on until she got off.

But crazy?

To me, she was the wisp of the wind's freedom,
a music-maker who once tried to teach me guitar
but ended up singing and singing,
me listening, and her singing
until I put the instrument down
and watched the clock click the lesson time away.

I didn't learn guitar, but I learned something
about her craving for the new, the unbroken,
so she could break it. Periodically she banished herself
from the family—and was the better for it.

I secretly admired Tía Chucha.
She was always quick with a story,
another "Pepito" joke or a hand-written lyric
that she would produce regardless of the occasion.

She was a despot of desire,
uncontainable as a splash of water
on a varnished table.

I wanted to remove the layers
of unnatural seeing,
the way Tía Chucha beheld
the world, with first eyes,
like an infant who can discern
the elixir within milk.

I wanted to be one of the prizes
she stuffed into her rumpled bag.

Night Dance—Watts 1975-78

Nothing in Watts whispers.
Every open window is a shout,
a night dance to a driving
pulse that crashes through
the broken walls of a Jordan Downs
second-floor flat.

Conga sounds and synthesizers
compete against the drunken
laughter and angry talk
of young crips whose world
is bigger than this place
but never as important.

Here innocence and terror
are woven into the summer
breeze as the cries of the
'hood deliver sacrifices
of sound and flesh,
as a mother's milk flows,

and the heat hangs on you
like a wet blanket.
All begins to blend, come apart
all is loving, destroying
while homegirls dance a jig
to a repertoire of police sirens.

The Concrete River

We sink into the dust, Baba and me,
Beneath brush of prickly leaves,
Ivy strangling trees—singing
Our last rites of *locura.*
Homeboys. Worshipping God-fumes
Out of spray cans.

Our backs press up against a corrugated steel fence
Along the dried banks of a concrete river.
Spray-painted outpourings on walls offer a chaos
Of color for the eyes.

Home for now. Hidden in weeds.
Furnished with stained mattresses
And plastic milk crates.
Wood planks thrust into thick branches
Serves as roof.
The door is a torn cloth curtain
(Knock before entering).
Home for now, sandwiched
In-between the maddening days.

We aim spray into paper bags.
Suckle them. Take deep breaths.
An echo of steel-sounds grates the sky.
Home for now. Along an urban-spawned
Stream of muck, we gargle in
The technicolored synthesized madness.

This river, this concrete river,
Becomes a steaming, bubbling
Snake of water, pouring over

Nightmares of wakefulness,
Pouring out a rush of birds
—a flow of clear liquid on a cloudless day.
Not like the black oil stains we lay in.
Not like the factory air engulfing us.
Not this plastic death in a can.

Sun rays dance on the surface.
Grey fish fidget below the sheen,
And us looking like Huckleberry Finns/
Tom Sawyers, with stick fishing poles,
As dew drips off low branches,
As if it was earth's breast milk.

Oh, we should be novas of our born days.
We should be scraping wet dirt with callused toes.
We should be flowering petals playing ball.

Soon water/fish/dew wane into a pulsating whiteness.
I enter a tunnel of circles, swimming toward
A glare of lights. Family and friends call to me:
I want to be there, in perpetual dreaming,
In the din of exquisite screams.
I want to know this mother-comfort
Surging through me.

I am a sliver of blazing ember entering a womb of brightness.
I am a hovering specter shedding scarred flesh.
I am a clown sneaking out of a painted mouth in the sky.
I am your son, 'ama, seeking the security of shadows
Fleeing weary eyes, bursting brown behind
A sewing machine.

I am your brother, the one you threw off rooftops,
Tore into with rage—the one you visited,
A rag of a boy, lying in a hospital bed, ruptured.

I am friend of books, prey of cops, lover of the barrio women
Selling hamburgers and tacos at the P&G Burger Stand.

I welcome this heavy shroud. I want to be buried in it,
To be sculptured marble in craftier hands.

Soon an electrified hum sinks teeth into brain.
Then claws surround me, pull at me,
Back to the dust, to the concrete river.

Let me go—to stay entangled
In this mesh of barbed serenity.
But over me is a face, mouth breathing back life.
I feel the gush of air, the pebbles and debris beneath me.

"Give me the bag, man," I slur.
"No way! You died, man," Baba said.
"You stopped breathing and died."
"I have to go back...you don't understand..."

I try to get up, to reach the sky.
Oh, for the lights—for this whore
of a sun to blind me, to entice me to burn.
Come back! Let me swing in delight
To the haunting knell, to pierce colors of virgin skies,
Not here along a concrete river,
But there—licked by tongues of flame.

The Rooster Who Thought It Was a Dog

Echo Park mornings came on the wings
of a rooster's gnawing squawk.
This noise, unfortunately, also brought in
the afternoon, evenings and most hours of the day.
The rooster had no sense of time
nor any desire to commit to one.
He cock-a-doodled whenever he had the notion.
For late sleepers, day sleepers or your plain,
ordinary, run-of-the-mill night sleepers,
annoyance had this rooster's beak.
It was enough to drive one nuts.
Often I opened my back window
that faced the alley just across from the backyard
where the rooster made his home.
"Shut up, or I'll blow your stinkin' brains out,"
I'd yell. Great communication technique.
It worked on the brats next door.
But the rooster never flinched.
With calm aplomb it continued to squawk.
For one thing the rooster never gave out
a bonifide cock-a-doodle. It sort of shouted it out.
It happened that the rooster lived with three dogs:
A German Shepherd and two mutts.
The dogs barked through their existence.
They barked at everything in sight.
I finally concluded:
That rooster thought it was a dog.
Somehow, I didn't mind the dogs barking,
but when a rooster barks...that's murder.
In fact, I often saw it running alongside
the dogs as they raced across the dirt yard

barking at passing cars and people.
If the dogs went left, the rooster went left.
They'd go right—and dang if the rooster
didn't go right as well.
Now I don't know if this is a regular condition
for roosters. I thought I had a story for
the "Weekly World News." I could see it now:
The Rooster Who Thinks It's A Dog.
Who knows what rooster dementia we had here?
And whether the rooster chased cats up trees
or pissed on fire hydrants, this wasn't clear.
But once I grasped the heart of the matter,
I began to see the rooster in another light.
I felt sorry for this fowl with an identity problem.
And I wondered how it must react when its
owners threw chicken bones to the dogs.
Would it nibble on the remains of its favorite hen?
I shuddered at the thought.
Yet despite the revelation of the rooster's bark,
the problem of sleep didn't end.
Then one day a new neighbor, a young lady,
who often drank herself to bliss,
grabbed a gun and blew the rooster away.
She became somewhat of a local hero,
I must say, though, it was an unfitting end
for the bird. But I suppose, one can tolerate barking dogs.
But barking roosters? That's another matter altogether.

Black Mexican

"The worse thing you can do is fall in love with a whore."
—A homeboy

"But she's a woman."
—Me

The girl appeared through the red haze
of stage lights, a black Mexican,
who told her family in Acapulco she was working
in Tijuana cleaning homes when in fact
she sold herself to sailors and tourists
reconquering the people on weekends.

She came to me, her small frame leaning
against a table, all of 15 years,
dark eyes shining through smoke.
Or I came to her, a teenaged runaway from *Lomas*,
hitchhiking into the void of antiquity,
needing more than the empty stares
of sunlight in the mirror.
Or she came to me, yearning for this dance
and the wraith of real love.

She walked up
with dreams of America
and yellowed teeth.
She came in the caricature of a voice,
with motherhood
sliced across her belly
and eyes of hiding in mud fields
as family sounds
closed in on her, carnivorous like dogs,
murmuring about how pretty she is,

how it doesn't hurt,
and the fathers,
the uncles
the brothers,
all slamming into her
until she could squeeze into herself
and die.

Across the way was a hotel of cracked plaster.
Its hallways echoed with the shouts of drunken boys,
blond like Ohio,
who scraped off the Tijuana women
from the soles of their feet.

We crossed the street
with the asphalt erupting beneath us,
and folded into a hotel room.
She undressed,
revealing the skin of ancient tribes;
still fighting, still bleeding.
I lay on the bed.
Told her no.
Told her yes.
Told her I had no money.
She looked at me as if sorry.
We exchanged fingers
then kissed, and I cried,
kissed and cried into the moments
of my first suckling.

The Bull's Eye Inn

Apologies to T.S. Eliot for the first two lines

Let us go then, you and I,
to the Bull's Eye Inn,
through the rusted iron gates
into the dark and damp, stepping on saw-dusted
floors gushing with ether, where my ex-wife
once waited tables on weekends grinning with death.
Come to where the blood, beer and barf
flowed with the bourbon washes.

My ex-wife often invited me to watch over her.
My job on those weekends, she explained,
was to sit in a dark corner by myself,
and keep the out-of-work mechanics,
the foundrymen and slow-talking *cholos*
from going too far—which was like
blowing a balloon and trying to stop before it burst.

Dudes would buy her drinks and she brought the drinks
over to me. Laid back against a plush seat,
I silently toasted their generosity.

I did a toast to her too, to our babies,
to the blood-shot eyes of East LA nights
and the midnight romps we once had,
near naked, in the park.

Many times in the candle-lit haze,
as a disc jockey played tunes behind a chain-link barrier,
the bullets came flying and the beer bottles
crashed on the wall behind my head.

Once on the dance floor some dude smacked his old lady
to the ground. Later that night she returned,
firing a .22 handgun into the bar
—and missing everybody—
as Little Willie G. crooned "Sad Girl"
from a turntable.

Con artists congregated here,
including the Earl of Lincoln Heights
who sold houses he didn't own.

And boys with tattoos and scars crisscrossing skin
prowled the pool tables, passing bills,
while trying to out-hustle each other
as disco beats and *cumbias* pulled people
onto the lopsided dance floor.

My ex-wife danced too. I watched dudes hold her,
kiss her neck, eye her behind
and look down her sweaty breasts.

But I also knew this was the closest
I would ever get to her anymore,
in that dark corner,
with beer bottles rising from a table
—when she needed me.

Outside the Bulls Eye Inn
the hurting never stopped.

Outside the Bulls Eye Inn
we locked into loathing
shrouded in the lips of love.

Outside the Bulls Eye Inn
we had two children
who witnessed our drunken brawls
—my boy once entered our room,
and danced and laughed with tears in his eyes
to get us to stop.

But inside, beside the blaze of bar lights,
she was the one who stole into my sleep,
the one who fondled my fears,
the one who inspired
the lust of honeyed remembrance.

She was the song of regret behind a sudden smile.

Waiting

What made the waiting so painful?
The woman had called: She was on her way.
Tense, I waited, sitting at the kitchen table.

There had been too many nights
waking up to bottles of booze and books on the floor,
two small children parked on blankets in a corner.

Alone ain't so bad.

Dreams of women yet to be touched,
to be smelled. It ain't bad.

Up on a hill, hidden by wood-and-shingle
shacks alongside curbless roads, visited by nobody
unless they had to be here.

Alone ain't so bad.

Hammering holes on walls with fists.
Tears streaming down my face at saxophone riffs.
Looking at old photos, feeding babies,
taking out trash and thinking of her.

It ain't so bad. I couldn't stand it.

Looked through personal ads in the weeklies.
Made phone calls. Wrote letters. Came across
Video-Date: "The God Send For Lonely People."
I called after three false starts. Lady said
she would be here Saturday.
It's Saturday and I'm climbing the walls.

Took an hour to find the place (an old stucco-white
basement room. You can't miss it:
Cholo graffiti on the front door).

She came, made her pitch, saw the hurt in my eyes
(I always spoke with my eyes, damn it), a longing
for sweet companionship—not of drunken homeboys
or angel-dusted street women. For the mother
of my kids, out at Sonny's Lounge, sucking Kahluas
and highballs while throwing out wicked smiles
at disco dudes.

The lady looked at my eyes—and then stopped.
Refused to sell me the Video-Date.
Refused to take the check.

"This can't help you," she said, and walked out.

Don't Read That Poem!

For Patricia Smith

She rises from a chair and slides toward the stage
with satin feet over a worn-wood floor.
She bears down on the microphone
like a blues singer about to reveal
some secrets. A fever of poems in her hand.
She seizes the mike and begins her seduction.

I'm in the back of the bar, my head down.
The things she does to me with words.
I want to leave. I want her never to begin.
She starts with a poem about Daddy-love
and I feel like getting up right there
and yelling: Don't read that poem!
That one that causes little bursts
of screams inside my head,
that makes tears come to my eyes,
that I refuse to let fall.

Don't read that poem!
The one about a daughter raped and killed
in the shadow of a second's dark fury.
I want to hide in the neon glare above me,
to swim away in the glass of beer
I hold close to me.
She does another poem
about her many mouths
and I want to howl:
Don't read that poem!
That one that entices me
to crawl under her skin,
to be her heartbeat.

Oh, how she plunks the right notes,
rendering me as clay in bruised hands.
No, don't do the one about
what it is to be a nine-year-old black girl,
the truth of it trembling at my feet.
Somebody should make her stop!

I should be home, watching TV,
blank-eyed behind stale headlines,
cold popcorn on the couch,
a dusty turntable going round and round and round.
I should be fixing a car. Or shooting eight-ball.
But I can't leave. I need to taste the salt of her soliloquy,
to be drunk with the sobriety
of her verse quaking beneath my eyelids.

Jarocho Blues

You came with long luxurious hair,
black as the deep tint of heart-blood,
almost blue.

You came with a smile and a guitar,
groping for a song:
Una nueva cancion.
Exitos de Augustin Lara.
Jarocho blues.

You came with a tequila bottle
and sat crossed-legged on a rug of colors.
I watched and you sang,
the lit air carried a litany
of women's stories.
Your voice a silk veil
over dripping candles,
bringing back family songs
over *copas de vino*.

Your voice and the night of day.

A mahogany wood table held an overturned glass.
You sat next to it and stretched the chords
over my eyes, strummed the strings
into infinity.

You sang and I fell into a notated dream
with a chorus of psalms drenched in sorrows.
You sang and the bougainvillea of youth
came to me in torrents. You sang
and tears cut a path down the wall,

blanketing me in a spell of ointments.
You sang and the tequila burned
the edges of my mouth.

I never wanted it to end, your singing.
A guitar across your lap. Your eyes closed.
Waves of hair over your shoulders
and strands stuck to sweat across your face.

You sang and I died. Dead for all the broken men.
Dead for all who ever stopped believing.
Dead for all who ever thought women
were less than the tint of this blood,
less than the warmth of our birth waters,
less than our deepest cry.

Dead for all who ever hungered to be touched
by the flesh of such a voice.

Jesus Saves

This dude *Jesus Saves* must be popular or something.
You see his name everywhere. I first saw it when I woke up
from a Bunker Hill cardboard box to a huge sign near the top
of the LA library. It read: "Jesus Saves."

I wish I were that guy. Then I wouldn't be
this chocked-faced pirate on city seas.
Then I wouldn't be this starved acrobat of the alcoves
loitering against splintered doors.
Then I wouldn't be this aberration
who once had a home, made of stone even,
and a woman to call wife.
In the old country I worked since I was seven.
I knew the meaning of the sun's behest
for pores to weep.
But now such toil is allowed
to rot like too many berries on a bush.

In the old country, I laughed the loudest,
made the most incisive remarks,
and held at bay even the most limpid of gatherings.

But here, I am a grieving poet, a scavenger of useless literature.
They mean nothing in this place...my metaphoric manner,
the spectacle of my viscous verse—nothing!
I am but a shadow on the sidewalk,
a spot of soot on a block wall; a roll of dice
tossed across a collapsing hallway in a downtown
single-room welfare hotel.

Okay, *Señor Saves*, right now this is your time.
But someday a billboard will proclaim my existence.
Someday people will sigh my name
as if it were confection on the lips.
As long as I have a rhythm in my breast,
there will come this fine day
when this orphan, pregnant with genius,
is discovered sprouting epiphanies like wings
on the doorstep of mother civilization.

The Blast Furnace

A foundry's stench, the rolling mill's clamor,
the jack hammer's concerto leaving traces
between worn ears. Oh sing me a bucket shop blues
under an accordion's spell
with blood notes cutting through the black air
for the working life, for the rotating shifts
for the day's diminishment and rebirth.
The lead seeps into your skin like rainwater
along stucco walls. It blends into the fabric of cells,
the chemistry of bone, like a poisoned paint brush
coloring skies of smoke, devouring like a worm
that never dies, a fire that's never quenched.
The blast furnace bellows out a merciless melody
as molten metal runs red down your back
as assembly lines continue rumbling
into your brain, into forever,
while rolls of pipes crash onto brick floors.
The blast furnace spews a lava of insipid dreams,
a deathly swirl of screams, of late night wars
with a woman, a child's book of fear,
a hunger of touch, a hunger of poetry,
a daughter's hunger for laughter.
It is the sweat of running, of making love,
a penitence pouring into ladles of slag.
It is falling through the eyes of a whore,
a red-core bowel of rot,
a red-eyed train of refugees,
a red-scarred hand of unforgiveness,
a red-smeared face of spit.
It is blasting a bullet through your brain,
the last dying echo of one who enters
the volcano's mouth to melt.

They Come To Dance

An aged bondo-spackled Buick
pushes dust around its wheels
as it slithers up Brooklyn Avenue
toward La Tormenta, bar and dance club.

The Buick pulls up to clutter
along a cracked sidewalk
beneath a street lamp's yellow luminance.
A man and a woman in their late 30s
pour out of a crushed side door.

They come to dance.

The man wears an unpressed suit and baggy pants:
K-Mart specials.
She is overweight
in a tight blue dress;
the slits up the side
reveal lace and panty hose.

They come with passion-filled bodies,
factory-torn like *ropa vieja*.
They come to dance the workweek away
as a soft rain buffets
the club's steamed windows.

Women in sharp silk dresses and harsh
painted on makeup crowd the entrance.
Winos stare at the women's flight across
upturned streets and up wooden stairs.

Men in slacks and cowboy shirts
or cheap polyester threads
walk alone or in pairs.

Oye compa, que onda pues?
Aqui no mas, de oquis. . .

Outside La Tormenta's doors
patrons line up to a van dispensing tacos
while a slightly-opened curtain
reveals figures gyrating
to a beat bouncing off strobe-lit walls.

They come to dance
and remember
the way flesh feels flush
against a cheek
and how a hand opens slightly,
shaped like a seashell,
in the small
of a back.

They come to dance
and forget
the pounding hum
of an assembly line
and the boss' grating throat
that tells everyone to go back to work
over the moans of a woman
whose torn finger dangles
in a glove.

They come to dance:
Former peasants. Village kings.
City squatters. High-heeled princesses.

The man and woman lock the car doors
and go through La Tormenta's weather-stained
curtain leading into curling smoke.

Inside the Buick are four children.
They press their faces
against the water-streaked glass
and cry through large eyes:
Mirrors of a distant ocean.

Carrying My Tools

Any good craftsman carries his tools.
Years ago they were always at the ready.
In the car. In a knapsack.
Claw hammers with crisscrossed heads,
32 ouncers. Wrenches in all sizes,
sometimes with oil caked on the teeth.
Screwdrivers with multi-colored
plastic handles (what needed screwing, got screwed).
I had specialty types: Allen wrenches,
torpedo levels, taps and dies.
A trusty tape measure.
Maybe a chalk line.
Millwrights also carried dial indicators,
Micrometers—the precision kind.
They were cherished like a fine car,
a bottle of rare wine
or a moment of truth.
I believed that anyone could survive
without friends, without the comfort of blankets
or even a main squeeze (for a short while anyway).
But without tools—now there was hard times.
Without tools, what kind of person could I be?
The tools were my ticket to new places.
I often met other travelers, their tools in tow,
and I'd say: Go ahead, take my stereo and TV.
Take my car. Take my toys of leisure.
Just leave the tools.
Nowadays, I don't haul these mechanical implements.
But I still make sure to carry the tools
of my trade: Words and ideas,
the kind no one can take away.

So there may not be any work today,
but when there is, I'll be ready.
I got my tools.

Bethlehem No More

For Bruce Springsteen

Bethlehem Steel's shift-turn whistles
do not blast out in Maywood anymore.

Mill workers no longer congregate
at Slauson Avenue bars on pay day.

Bethlehem's soaking pits are frigid now.

Mill families, once proud and comfortable,
now congregate for unemployment checks or food.

Bethlehem, I never thought you would be missed.
When we toiled under the girders, we cursed your name.

But you were bread on the table, another tomorrow.

My babies were born under the Bethlehem health plan.
My rent was paid because of those long and humid days and nights.

I recall being lowered into oily and greasy pits
or standing unsteady on two-inch beams

thirty feet in the air and wondering if I would survive

to savor another weekend.
I recall my fellow workers who did not survive,

burned alive from caved-in furnace roofs
or severed in two by burning red steel rods

while making your production quotas.

But Bethlehem you are no more. We have made you rich,
rich enough to take our toil and invest it elsewhere.

Rich enough to make us poor again.

Every Road

Every road should come to this end:
A place called home.
When you don't have one
the expanse of sky is your roof,
the vast fields of green your living room.
Every city, your city.
When you speak, you speak for the country.
In the wrinkled faces and the sun-scarred eyes,
mother earth calls us to fury.
Every child without a home
is everyone's child.
The daily murders go unanswered:
To die of cold in sunny California.
To starve in New York City,
the restaurant capital of the world.
To have no coat on the Broadway of coats.
The crimes pile up as high as the mountains
of grain that are warehoused and stored away
from those who need it.
A mother's child is taken away for neglect
because she can't pay rent and eat at the same time.
Children born of a labor of love are condemned
for the lack of labor.
Every road should come to this end.
A place called home.

Every Breath, a Prayer

San Quintin, Baja California, Mexico 1983

Fernando, *el mixteco*, climbs the red dirt
of Baja hills along rain-drenched paths
and wades through fields of waist-high grass.
He stops at a clearing where a rainbow of piled stones
colored sticks and flowers share communion
with the ground of the living
to the ground of the dead.

Dozens of baby graves fill the hillside:
Little ones in shoebox-sized coffins
adorned with painted rock, sea shells
and wooden crosses, sprinkled with dry leaves.
They are buried near the tomato plants
where some 80,000 *Mixteco* Indians
are seasonally enslaved.

Fernando, *el mixteco*, leaves his plastic and carton shack
and passes an old irrigation pump where his three-year-old
son was crushed in the mesh of steel gears
on a Sunday of play.

Fernando crisscrosses the sutured earth
alongside the fires that light the glazed faces
of mothers squatting with diseased children
in the heart of dust.

He steps across a rotting plank
used as a bridge over a stream
as a woman leans over, pushing rags
wet against the rocks, and another nearby
pressing a crusted nipple to the mouth
of a baby—its every breath, a prayer.

Fernando, *el mixteco*, then eyes the north
where a wind comes and ruffles his thick hair
as he declares death to death,
his eyes dark with the hollow
of unborn days.

Fernando's body becomes the sides
of a native dirt-brick house,
his hair turns into a tarred-paper
and branched roof
—an arm becomes a child becomes home.

Lips

I sat in Chicago traffic
waiting for a light to change.
My fingers scored a rhythm
on top of the metal door
while faces stared down
from third-floor bay windows.
Not to intrude, but from behind a blue Toyota
I spotted them. Lips.
Perfect, red, with thin creases
and slightly opened.
Lips like candy
encased in a rectangular side-view mirror.
My car was just behind the Toyota.
The back of a woman's head in front of me.
But in the mirror just lips, enormous
as they rubbed the sides of the plastic rim.
The lips took off after the next green.
I pressed the accelerator,
unmindful of the old lady trying
to cross the street
with bags on both arms.
I was compelled to look at those lips
even as they rushed through a yellow light
forcing me to risk the red.
The lips carried with them
the soul of skin,
the summer of a smile, taking me home.
Lips like being cradled in a soft rain,
making me do a perfect back flip
into wet memory.
Lips whispering into my ear,
licking the side of my mouth,

hiding secrets behind honeyed faces.
It didn't matter what the woman looked like.
She had lips.
Then the turn signals flashed
and lips made a left-hand turn.
I continued on over the ruptured streets,
thinking of lips
through the flames of afternoon traffic.

from
Trochemoche – 1998

Meeting the Animal in Washington Square Park

The acrobats were out in Washington Square Park,
flaying arms and colors—the jokers and break
dancers, the singers and mimes. I pulled out
of a reading at New York City College
and watched a crowd gather around a young man
jumping over 10 garbage cans from a skateboard.
Then out of the side of my eye I saw someone
who didn't seem to belong here, like I didn't
belong. He was a big man, six feet and more,
with tattoos on his arms, back, stomach and neck.
On his abdomen were the words in huge old English
lettering: *Hazard*. I knew this guy, I knew that place.
I looked closer. It had to be him. And it was—Animal!
From East L.A. World heavyweight contender.
The only Chicano from L.A. ever ranked
in the top ten of the division. The one who
went toe to-toe with Leon Spinks and even
made Muhammad Ali look the other way.
Animal! I yelled. "Who the fuck are you?" he asked,
a quart of beer in his grasp, eyes squinting.
My name's Louie—from East L.A. He brightened. "East L.A.!
Here in Washington Square Park? Man, we everywhere!"
Then the proverbial "what part of East L.A.?" came next.
But I gave him a shock. From *La Geraghty*, I said.
That's the mortal enemy of the Big Hazard
gang. "I should kill you," Animal replied.
Hey, if we were in L.A., I suppose you would
—but we in New York City, man.
"I should kill you anyway."
Instead he thrust out his hand with the beer and offered
me a drink. We talked—about what had happened since he stopped
boxing. About the time I saw him at the Cleland House
arena looking over some up-and-coming fighters.

How he had been to prison and later ended up homeless
in New York City, with a couple of kids somewhere.
And there he was, with a mortal enemy from East L.A.,
talking away. I told him how I was now a poet,
doing a reading at City College, and he didn't wince
or looked surprised. Seemed natural. Sure. A poet
from East L.A. That's the way it should be. Poet
and boxer. Drinking beer. Among the homeless,
the tourists and acrobats. Mortal enemies.
When I told him I had to leave, he said "go then,"
but soon shook my hand, East L.A. style, and walked off.
"Maybe, someday, you'll do a poem about me, eh?"
Sure, Animal, that sounds great.
Someday, I'll do a poem about you.

Victory, Victoria, My Beautiful Whisper

For Andrea Victoria

You are the daughter who is sleep's beauty.
You are the woman who birthed my face.
You are a cloud creeping across the shadows,
drenching sorrows into heart-sea's terrain.
Victory, Victoria, my beautiful whisper,
how as a baby you laughed into my neck
when I cried at your leaving
after your mother and I broke up;
how at age three you woke me up from stupid
so I would stop peeing into your toy box
in a stupor of resentment and beer;
and how later, at age five, when I moved in
with another woman who had a daughter about your age,
you asked: "How come *she* gets to live with Daddy?"

Muñeca, these words cannot traverse the stone
path of our distance; they cannot take back the thorns
of falling roses that greet your awakenings.
These words are from places too wild for hearts to gallop,
too cruel for illusions, too dead for your eternal
gathering of flowers. But here they are, weary offerings
from your appointed father, your anointed man-guide;
make of them your heart's bed.

Catacombs

The concave view over desert groves
    is maligned, dense with sacrifices
    not to be believed.
A native face peers backward to time
    and woman, gathering memory like
    flowers on healing cactus.
Your eye is froth & formation, it is
    rain of protocol you can't relinquish
    as water is wasted on sacred sand.

Across the turquoise rug, hexagon shapes.

I discover you, the howl of eternal mornings
    while beckoning the blue from this sky,
    while gesturing an infant from sleeping tree.
Sip the maguey juice from these mountains,
    shear chaos from the catacombs:
    forget and ferment the pain.

On the back of your hand, circles of flame.

to the police officer who refused to sit in the same room as my son because he's a "gang banger"

For Ramiro

How dare you!
How dare you pull this mantle from your soiled
sleeve and think it worthy enough to cover my boy.
How dare you judge when you also wallow in this mud.
Society has turned over its power to you,
relinquishing its rule, turned it over
to the man in the mask, whose face never changes,
always distorts, who does not live where I live,
but commands the corners, who does not have to await
the nightmares, the street chants, the bullets,
the early-morning calls, but looks over at us
and demeans, calls us animals, not worthy
of his presence, and I have to say: How dare you!
My son deserves to live as all young people.
He deserves a future and a job. He deserves
contemplation. I can't turn away as you.
Yet you govern us? Hear my son's talk.
Hear his plea within his pronouncement,
his cry between the breach of his hard words.
My son speaks in two voices, one of a boy,
the other of a man. One is breaking through,
the other just hangs. Listen, you who can turn away,
who can make such a choice—you who have sons
of your own, but do not hear them!
My son has a face too dark, features too foreign,
a tongue too tangled, yet he reveals, he truths,
he sings your demented rage, but he sings.
You have nothing to rage because it is outside of you.
He is inside of me. His horror is mine. I see what

he sees. And if my son dreams, if he plays, if he smirks in the mist of moon-glow, there I will be, smiling through the blackened, cluttered and snarling pathway toward your wilted heart.

A Tale of Los Lobos

One summer, to watch Los Lobos play,
I drove several hundred miles
from Chicago to Charleston,
West Virginia with three
Chicano buddies: Geronimo,
Mitch and Dario.
We got there in time to catch
a great concert. Afterwards,
we went backstage and talked
to the band members.
We told the band we'd see them
later at the honky tonk club
where they were expected to perform.
But they had to leave right away
and couldn't make it.
We arrived at the club, sans Lobos,
and the place was packed.
I didn't think there'd be a seat,
but soon someone directed us to a table
where three pitchers of beer stood
at attention on the varnished table top.
Great service, I thought. We sat down,
poured beers into frosty glasses,
and took in the down-home blues
emanating from the small, smoke-filled stage.
Before we finished the pitchers,
three more were brought over
(although nobody had asked for our money).
So we drank away, enjoying ourselves,
the only Mexicans in the place.
What gives? I asked. Geronimo, Mitch and Dario
shrugged their shoulders.

Soon many eyes turned our way.
Something's up, I whispered,
look at the way everybody's looking at us.
Sure enough, the band stopped and someone
at the mike asked us to come up to the stage.
"¡Que cabula!" Mitch exclaimed, "they think
we're Los Lobos!"
Damn, man, I said, we don't even look like them!
Geronimo stood up, said he was sorry
but we weren't Los Lobos, and sat down.
Everything stopped. Incredulous stares
surrounded us. After an embarrassing
silence, the house band began
a slow number, than upped the tempo,
finally rocking the place
with harmonica-laden fervor.
Hijo de su, they believe us, I said.
"I don't know," Dario replied,
"I think they think we're lying."
One dude approached us:
"I know you're Los Lobos;
you just don't want to play, right?"
No, for reals, we ain't them, I responded.
He winked and kept on walking.
When I went to the restroom,
a woman by the phone stopped me:
"I liked the way you played guitar
at the gig earlier."
That wasn't me, I explained.
"What I want to know," the girl then asked,
"is how you got rid of the goatee so fast."
I took my piss and rushed back to my seat.
Rumors that we were Los Lobos abounded.
Some shouted for us to get off it and perform.
"If we did," Geronimo quipped, "Los Lobos
would never play this town again."

I then noticed a bevy of West Virginia beauties,
local groupies, who followed the out-of-town
bands that landed here. They wouldn't leave
even after we gave them expressions that said:
you're nice, but we ain't them!
One girl who sat directly behind me
had on a prom dress! She kept
ordering gin-and-tonics, waiting for a signal
from one of us, I presumed, for her
to join us at the table. We decided not to go
this route. Mitch figured we might have to scram
if people here concluded we had
insulted their fair city, club and women.
All our denials seemed pointless,
resulting in more knowing winks
as if they were all in on our little joke.
The pitchers kept coming,
the house band coaxed us up
once or twice,
and the groupies held on
like real troupers.
Finally, people began to depart.
The band packed up its instruments
and most of the girls had split.
Then just before our last beer,
a loud thump exploded behind me.
I turned. The girl in the party dress
had fallen over in her chair,
drunker than shit! We helped her back
on the stool. My partners and I
promptly left the club as quietly as we could
on the night Los Lobos didn't play
in Charleston, West Virginia.

Woman on the First Street Bridge

Traffic crawled for miles in front of me
and a similar number of miles behind.
Sandwiched between a truck-bed piled
with oil-soaked auto parts and a crumpled sedan,
I felt like melting beneath the peppered sun
as I inhaled the fetid fumes, scratched
my steaming eyeballs and crept toward
the concrete bridge facing the jagged skyline.
I had been on a work prowl, hiking up and down
factory row next to the housing projects
that lined the east side of the Los Angeles River.
I passed soot-stained brick walls and opened
creaky warehouse doors that sang a chorus
of "no work today" as heartbreaking
as a woman's rejections.

For hours I closed in on secretaries,
bored to their toes, and filled out applications
that were later piled on top of hundreds
with names and personal statistics similar to mine.
Finally, too tired to continue, I sank into my car seat
and entered the crest of blaring vehicles,
feeling like a coffin sliding toward a crematory furnace.

The sun's rays beat malicious against the car's metal top.
Sweat simmered on skin. My breath rose in short gasps.
Then something happened that was as refreshing
as a Tecate beer in the Death Valley desert:
A woman, who stood at the entrance
of the First Street bridge,
lifted her dress to her neck,
revealing dark nipples on a mass of breasts

and masturbated to an open-mouthed
audience of imprisoned procession.

She must have known what we were going through
—she must have known what sorcery
could snap us out of it.

The Rabbi and the Cholo

The Rabbi appeared, black dressed and uncertain,
like a shadow of doubt. My world
then was perfectly squared: I was at war
with humanity, the Rabbi indistinguishable
from the enemy. I had the world
between my teeth,
scratching at betrayed skies,
seeking deliverance in mortar and brick,
behind tattered sneers.
I shifted the firmament
through thick fingers,
dust in the grooves of skin,
between eyes,
between sighs.

The Rabbi's words broke through
hatred's mask, peeling into
something calm, soft.
He spoke for the centuries:
Of nomadic sons, Hebrew invocations,
desert songs and tattooed numbers.
The Rabbi carried everything for everybody.
He said he feared me, that he had to know me.
His fear and my hatred somehow
found fugue and notation,
music and reverberation.

Rabbi and Cholo—the distance as great
as those between L.A. settlements,
different countries really.
He listened to my stories
like a voyeur of myths: Stories of scaled fences,
of stray bullets between blemished palm trees,

of failed robberies and failed courage,
of carnal intimacies with women
dark as me, risking all for the voice
to wrap the flesh like perpetual rain.
The Rabbi and the Cholo. We strolled
the callused streets, across ravines and hills,
through back roads of mud
and rotting cars, places he never knew,
taking in the stinging odors
of urine stains on stucco walls,
of *carnitas* at midnight stalls,
of bloodied roosters in cages
and love-drunk men groping at running ballads
lamenting loss between shots
of earth-born tequila.

I waded through Fairfax corridors,
through hatted men in ancient
arguments, through bagel shops and Synagogue
doorways, dazed at the Mediterranean
gazes of girls and their well-dressed
Brentwood mothers. I stood there
in starched baggy Khaki pants and Pendelton
flannel shirt, buttoned only at the top,
with bandanna and skull cap above my eyes,
among the bearded Semite faces
in black pants and suits, who appeared
like 1920s Lower East Side
or Boyle Heights: Nothing here
but escape,
exile and escape.

One night, at a "brotherhood" camp, the Rabbi
witnessed me break down, for the first time
since I was eleven: I mourned for all
the dead homies, for the women who walked,

for family and the wounds of silence.
The Rabbi sat down next to me and said:
"I don't know how to cry like that."

The Rabbi and the Cholo:
There was no closing of parting waters here.
I was laughter and sun, vessel
of swollen tales, someone who could shout
when enough is never enough:
My inner-life was close to the touch;
the Rabbi had his layered beneath
charcoal cloth, tradition, voices...
plea and birthright.

One summer we gazed at the ocean
that caressed Venice Beach.
I focused on the waves,
the froth, the wreckage of sea;
the Rabbi took in the deep lull
and blue mass at the distance.
In a hasty moment, on that moist shore,
severed from history, I responded
as if this "too will pass."
The issues were immediate, my enemies close,
nothing vast like time:
My grief was simple then, pure,
Definite—now.
The Rabbi was nothing if not history,
time for him an immense divide;
his grief, forever.

Cinco de Mayo

Cinco de Mayo celebrates a burning people,
those whose land is starved of blood,
civilizations that are no longer
holders of the night. We reconquer with our feet,
with our tongues, that dangerous language,
saying more of this world than the volumes
of textured and controlled words on a page.
We are the gentle rage. Our hands hold
the steam of the earth, the flowers
of dead cities, the green of butterfly wings.
Cinco de Mayo is about the barefoot, the untooled,
the warriors of want who took on the greatest army
Europe ever mustered—and won.
I once saw a Mexican man stretched across
an upturned sidewalk
near Chicago's 18th and Bishop one fifth of May day.
He brought up a near-empty bottle
to the withering sky and yelled out a *grito*
with the words: *¡Que viva Cinco de Mayo!*
And I knew then what it meant
—what it meant for barefoot Zapoteca *indigenas*
in the Battle of Puebla and what it meant for me
there on 18th Street among *los ancianos*,
the moon-faced children and futureless youth
dodging gunfire and careening battered cars,
and it brought me to that war,
that never ends, the war Cinco de Mayo
was a battle of, that I keep fighting,
that we keep bleeding for, that war
against our servitude that a *compa*
on 18th Street knew all about
as he crawled inside a bottle of the meanest
Mexican spirits.

Civilization

"I am tired of building up somebody else's civilization"
—Fenton Johnson

There are days when sunshine is toxic, when breathing becomes fatal
and the love stares of innocence have fangs. There are days
when caresses are lethal drumming and the low murmur of a child's
voice is a hand slap of hell flames across my face;
when all civilization is a squabble in my partner's
gaze and morality is a gun at my head. I didn't make this place.
So what if I say you can eat it! Eat it and choke. This heart-a-choke,
this diet of hypocrisies, this horse feed of fed horses. This salt seasoning
all wounds. Tear it down! Then wake me up when it's over.
Should I care if you don't care? Should I sweat the details when
the whole enchilada reeks? Just because you wear a hat and call
that fashion? Because you love the prison and hate the alien?
Don't come to me whining about your lost glories—they are the lashes
on slave skin, the gold stolen off the blanket of stones
called our land; they are the tongues cut from wiser heads, the deflowered,
dehydrated sirens that called you, then were slaughtered.
Don't cry for me Argentina—or Pennsylvania for that matter.
You say I'm no good, but my pathologies are what's keeping me
from cutting your throats.
All enslavers. All exploiters. All engravers of God-money.
You who see my children and go insane,
who wear the flesh of Nahuas like shiny suits,
who have Black Hills in your nightmares,
who eat with Che's severed hands,
who feed your wives to dogs on cracked plates,
who provide heroin to chiseled daughters,
who bathe in the Trail of Tears,
who sell tickets to the Middle Passage,
whose academies hold literature hostage,

whose culture crumbles in the hand
of a glue-sniffing Chicano child.

Fire

For Eduardo Galeano

1.

It seems our days are shaped by conflagration.
Felice, a poet from Chicago, recalls
the sugar canes of Santo Domingo
—black acrid taste in the Caribbean sun.

I remember Oaxaca where flames swirled
around a row of carved steer heads, eyes boiling,
as an Indian hand tears off
muscle and meat for tacos.

And then also Managua where tires
kindle, arousing an odor akin to acid,
to protest Contra raids
or another injustice.

African drums. Indigenous flutes.
Gypsies and a deep song.
Their rhythms rise like steam,
fueled by an earth *elumbrada.*

Fire follows us like family,
like the rivers of revolt
in San Salvador, Leon and Chiapas,
forever traced in mind.

2.

In Chicago, depressed neighborhoods
are dotted with vacant lots like missing
teeth in an old man's mouth as buildings
are torched for insurance claims.

Consuming blaze once stormed through a three-flat
in the barrio of Pilsen.
Men, women & children poured out doors,
jumped out windows, some with clothes clinging on flesh.

They accounted for all the occupants except
a 12-year-old boy; a father paced frantic
as firefighters drenched a collapsing roof.
For three days crews scoured the scorch.

Neighbors held a vigil as soaked and charred
walls crumbled in the search. And every
morning the alderman waited outside,
his own little girl in arms.

When finally city workers pulled
the boy out of the ruins, hundreds hushed
as he appeared among them, this *mestizaje*
devoured by the hell-spawn that never ceases

to stir us, to smolder in our breasts,
as fire becomes the luminous dawn,
the squeeze of skin, this memory
called our history.

Red Screams

After a talk with Michael Meade

The girl who used razors
to slash the length of her arms
called the opened flesh "red screams."
They are the mouths
of all our silences,
for what we can only imagine.
They are the vowels
in octave spiral
toward our fears.
Listening is not enough.
What bass fluctuates
in the resounding pangs
between these ears?
If we get near
let the rhythm speak,
convulsing beneath our caresses.
We may not understand
but I think about this:
If violins could stay our hands,
we'd all learn to play.

A Fence of Lights

A row of lights on asphalt
serves as fence between two buildings
separating them
keeping them on their margins of space
the fence gropes in symmetry
as snowflakes descend
like an obscure whiteness dancing
lightly before my gaze
everything is clouded in a density
of winter-screen
as in a memory or painting
while impressions saunter through
as this unfocusing allows me to see
something else about light
about colors
about structure
how the weather is tied to what I see
how what I see is pushing out what I feel
how what I feel becomes what matters
not the flakes, not the row of lights
like fences, not this gravel walk
but the inescapable light-dance of senses

Next Generation

There is a death sentence
poised above the boys
who, even now, straddle
the razor edge of living and dying.
And what of the girls?
They try so hard
only to end up as mothers
to the fathers
who mutate the daughters.

At Quenchers Bar When You Said Goodbye

When I sink into your waters,
I only know drowning.
I forget when we started to talk again
as one forgets the first time
one spoke as a child.
But every time we argue
and then get back together
we are like two legs
parting
to give birth.

The Face on the Radio

Helicopters hover like hellish hogs
of Armageddon:
An infra-red shakedown.
We are the enemy, the face on the radio,
burnt petals cluttering the sidewalk.
We are daylight's demise, dancing between
discord & distrust. All is bitter harvest,
betrayal and bewilderment;
all is seed for the fields of retreat:

bullets now punctuate every poem.

The Object of Intent Is To Get There

"I am in the world to change the world."
—Muriel Rukeyser

One lifetime meets another lifetime
in a constant lifetime of wars.
Leaning cities greet us at every station
and every wound points to the same place.
If your unique pain cancels out my unique pain
then there is nothing unique about pain.
What's left to do
but carry your troubles to where they're going;
once there, you stumble on the rest of us.

Untouched

A tequila bottle is perched
in the pantry, untouched,
next to the vinegar,
a sticky container of corn syrup
& an unopened can of black olives.
Visitation is sweet;
now only the aroma
stings the fingers.

A Father's Lesson

My mother warned
my brother and I
how my father
was going to punish us
for having pictures of nude women
under our mattress.
Anticipation was intense.
Finally, when the *viejo* came home,
he glanced at the photos,
gave us a short stern talk,
sent us to our rooms
then calmly placed the pictures
inside his shirt pocket.

Francisca

Untimely visions of you
while driving into a cloud.
All I remember
is jagged glass
and many regrets
balanced across
your glossed lips.

Suburbia

"Oppression makes even God smell foul."
—Felipe Luciano

Reading the newspaper I feel like an accomplice;
a voyeur is also guilty of something.
So the murders, the corruptions
and calculated larcenies against the spirit
reside in me too.
It's easy, I suppose, to pretend
I don't pay rent to the conspiracies.
And that the church is immune
because it's tax exempt.
But from a landfill or cemetery
grow multi-colored flowers.
Who can say then
from what polluted soils
my blossoms will spring?

Believe me when I say...

water is the skin of the earth
trains are arteries with corpuscles of people
a sigh is an ancestor praying
 woman's body is suspended over the land
tears come from clouds in your head
writing a poem is like fathering a river
waiting is the art of desire
something about a city makes you want to kill
fetuses scribble on the walls of wombs

Reflection on El Train Glass

Gaze penetrates through the glass
of El train window. It infringes
& infiltrates, a misdemeanor
against silence. I turn toward it.
The face in the haze refracting glare
in myriad directions, slicing into
working woman's tiredness, into
child's affront, into uniformed
man's wariness, into the uninterested
below city still-life.

A vise of sun rays grips a shape,
an innuendo of myself.
A caress of shade on the cheek.
I'm recalling the places I've been,
like flesh below the waters of a bath,
and I sleep into this transparent
world, sleep into a sort of flying,
into molds of day, into cinders
and the feel that doesn't feel
—into a stupor deeper than reflection.

The Quiet Woman

The quiet woman roams in the din of belly screams.
She knows rivers and caves and curbsides.
She knows the advent of furled fists.
She is the quiet woman, shadow on park bench,
pushed into needle grass, a disheveled syllable
uttered between makeshift schemes. The burden
of memories is the salvage of fantasy flames,
the mossed-faced whose stare streams through stria.
Here comes the quiet woman, a blossom in the womb of night.
The miracle-pulp in her hands. She swerves
around odors of hurt, odors of neglect,
of treachery and a lie. What's the scent of a poem?
The quiet woman knows; she breathes it in
and exhales. Others take the naturalism away,
remove the tender. All that's left is facade
and caricature. All veneer and word play.
But for a quiet woman, a poem is a smile so open
she's afraid of falling in.

Questions for Which You Are Always the Answer

For Maria Trinidad, "La Trini"

Whose Jalisco harangues the Jalisco in my stroll,
who lays across the ruins of Teotihuacan like rainwater,
whose face outlines the bathroom walls of *cantinas*,
who is the *aguardiente* that tongues my coarse throat?
What sleep becomes the dexterous hand of memory,
what skin is the lodestone of desire,
what song is fusion between a woman's walk and sunrise,
what drunkenness befalls while falling into those native eyes,
what stitching collects the shreds of midnight silence?
Who says what only solace can say,
what only mariachi's horns and good mescal can vanquish?
What bones lift this face to a face of lovely bones,
what moist fingers straighten the collars of qualms,
what evening wind arouses the color in blood,
pretending the wet in water—what voice is chocolate icing?
How deep are the potholes of lust,
how necessary is the milk of that touch,
how perpetual is the distance of thighs,
how vaginal is the soul's vortex?
Trini, you know what I can't know
—what tempest gathers in my lungs.

"Eva sitting on the curb with pen and paper before the torturers came to get her"

After a conversation with P.Z.

The phone call came on a night of a bruising
battle with my computer, writhing out some
scalding word-art. It was from a man who
claimed to be the "King of Poetry."
His first words were: "Are you beauty who
wants to be true?" And I thought, sure, why not?
People have said worse.
"I am king because I understand
eternal harmony with infinite beauty,"
he continued. And who was I to argue?
"Truth cannot be against the lie; the lie
is against the truth." I was with him so far.
Then he spoke about Eva, a perfect
poet, he claimed, "an angel born for it,"
and how she was "incarnate ecstasy,
light of the absolute." He kept on
with reminisces, fragments,
and epiphanies, including one about
a seven-year-old Mexican girl
he spotted from a fire escape in Pilsen:
"They will kill her before she is 17,"
he declared. And I agreed—this, too, is true.
He talked about writing a book for the
universal child, how he had eclipsed
his Italian background to be human,
and how those youth in jail "love death to be
with the dead ones who can't hurt them."
He appeared to surpass even this,
the real, the cold, the brutal

tongues licking us to sleep. Here was a Dante
for our times, whose mythical Eva
rouses poetry from its quilted slumber.
Here was a concrete Buddha challenging
even me to drink from the chalice of my own gifts.
"You are on your knees—stand up!" he yelled
before hanging up, his words like wings to cross
the battered skies of all illiteracies.

¡Seguro Que Hell Yes!

Apologies to Flaco Jimenez

We have passed this way before,
laden with sod, skeleton tongues
marking the dark. We have eaten of this
dust, we have scraped it off our faces,
we have dreamed this wound, this world
of vileness *tantas veces* that it's a song
beneath our breathing. *¡Seguro Que Sí!*
We knew it was coming before it came.
Ya hemos pasado por este camino,
and venom eyes seek us, taunting
mouths greet us. The most rooted people
of the land are the most revered
and the most despised, making us myths
even as mother earth daily births us.
We cross many borders and cross
into ourselves. This America
that Emerson called a poem
is a barbed wire. Our sweat, our blood,
and the *lagrimas* shed for thee,
are fashioned into a prison.
Freedom for some is slavery for me.
Whenever they lie a part of us
is murdered. This we know, and our
children cannot let it be. This we know,
and we challenge our skins to take it on.
This we know because we have passed
this way before, *sequro que sí*, cactus
bedding at our feet, snake curling through
our limbs. *Ya hemos pasado por este camino*,
and we can never stop coming.

The desert calls us: The fire-scarred trees,
the dried bones of elders, the silent screaming
of stones, they call us back
and we come, because we have died so many
times to the sun, because we belong
to the rivers wild, because
we never feared the blue
in the eye, the green in the heart,
the searing laws and guns and lies,
because we dreamed all this,
and now we are awake to dream again.
¡*Seguro que* hell yes!

Poem for Shakespeare & Company

For George Whitman and his great book store in Paris
on the occasion of a fire, July 18, 1990, which destroyed
much of the store's Sylvia Beach Library

There is a burnt room
above the Shakespeare & Co. bookstore:
A library once full of books
now ash. It speaks of how
books burn so well,
the pulp and cloth ablaze
like great forest fires.
But George Whitman knows
books burn bright without flame.
Every voice at Shakespeare and Company
is the hum of minds ablaze in books.
And Whitman has books to kill for.

At the Tumbleweed Hotel
there are books and faces on every wall.
There are photos of Whitman
with the fiery eyes of revolution.
These are books and faces
that are humanity's
hobbled steps toward heaven.
Here words swirl around me
as fire does around a book.
And I know: I am
the pulp and cloth these walls
were meant to engulf.

¡Yo Voy Ami!

For Arlene Osuna and the people of Humboldt Park, Chicago

Tuck-pointed brick scrapes up against dead branches with
    weathered gray backstairs and alleys scrawled with breath;

these are nights of girls shrieking, of drunken men in
    muddled Spanish, pulling women out of their depths;

these are nights of young couples, newly-wed poor,
    threatening to pay rent while an eruption of semi-

automatics welcomes them and Toyota hatchbacks
    cruise by with large speakers out the back, thumping Street

Mixes, and decals of *Yo Voy Ami* and *Soy
Boricua* on their windows. *Así y asa.*

Tri-colored flags are sold at the edge of *el parque*
    Humboldt next to Pentecostals enticing sinners

and housewives to open-air tents while a live band
    jump-starts the vibes in their chests and peddlers prepare

mofongo and *piraguas* for the shift-changing
    gente de trabajo; children race ahead of their

mothers who are busy *averiguando la mortificación*
    of life to neighbors with homemade *pasteles*

in paper sacks; police detour traffic for summer
    block parties as fire hydrants with inner tubes wrapped

around the openings blast relief to the shorties
        browning beneath a searing sun; nearby, my teenage

neighbor, with a prosthetic foot after the real
        one had been accidentally shot off when she

was three, calls over thirteen-year-old Arlene,
        who sometimes watches over my one-year-old son,

who's barely able to walk yet is fast when one
        isn't looking. *Así y asa*. Two years later Arlene

is killed when a bullet meant for her boyfriend claims
        her instead. Mingo next door has chickens and roosters

in the backyard. He dreams of Ponce in its breezes
        yet lures part of the island to Mozart Street.

My Jamaican neighbor also yearns for Caribbean
        waters, but his Alabama-born wife only

misses the open spaces of her home; some time
        later we see their sons in the juvenile

court when my oldest boy has a hearing at the
        same time. One day a coffee-colored dove lands

on my head outside my front door. It ambles to my
        shoulder and stays there. I end up getting a cage

and keeping it for a few days until the constant
        cooing and spurts of dove wails grate on my nerves.

I finally had it with the bird when my wife
        and I almost come to blows over whether we should

cover the cage to keep it quiet. I give the damn
    thing to Mingo. On hot weekends, neighbors aim

speakers out their windows while others then push out
    their own sounds and the competing salsa permeates

the street while local drug dealers appear with school-age
    boys as look-outs. After a while, I don't mind the

racket outside, but just don't have a faucet leak
    in the kitchen or I go nuts. *Así y asa.*

Oh Arlene, sweet Arlene, with straight burnished hair and
    luminous eyes, with wisps of girl legs and morning

sacraments of smile, framed by wrought iron fences.
    Bendita, you deserved more than this world would give!

Rant, Rave & Ricochet

Police killed her brother
for stealing a piece of chicken;

she says there's nothing
to do but squat. She's had

babies this way. Some nothing
more than arteries,

gray matter and fluid.
Three came out all right

and were taken away
by bureaucrats. She's homeless.

She's been raped and almost killed.
They say she's mad. For her,

sanity is a crime.
"I'm not stuck on stupid,"

she exclaims, and welcomes the
chaos which crackles out

of social construct. It's
her only peace in the

piece of the street at war.
She rants & raves, but it's all

ricochet from the bullet
that has claimed her since birth.

She pulls at strands of hair
flooding a furrowed face,

declares herself twine,
thimble and an ace of hearts.

Cloth of Muscle and Hair

Pink oily bodies hang on a line
like cloth of muscle and hair.
Flayed in rapid order with a delicate slice
of pelt, they are held by their feet, their skin
pulled from the flesh, down toward the damp
ground. The five-year-old girl wept, having held
these same rabbits only a day before,
gathering them close, fur to face, stroking them
and sensing their pulse beneath her fingers.
My Greek neighbor had done this for years,
raising rabbits to die, and displaying them
on a nylon wire to sell to other neighbors.
The girl's tears failed to spark in him
a gnawing nightmare of wet body parts
lurching through late night foam,
creeping up the back while wailing out
our mortality, proving we are no less
flayable, with emotions ripped
from the muscles of psyche. Nothing
stirred the panic from my neighbor's hand
even as the girl ran into the house,
unable to bear the dead rabbits,
with their furred feet intact,
speaking to her of how soft things can lose
their mild yielding, how they can become
creatures of clawed meat, become objects
that invade wretched memory when something,
anything, pushes out the soft white sheath
of innocence.

The Old Woman of Mérida

The old woman stares out an open window,
shards of sunlight pierce her face
cutting shadows on skin. She is washing
her hands after the dishes, dipping them
into a sea of hues and shapes,
a sea of syllables without sound,
in a stone house in Mérida,
her Mérida of dense Mexico.

The water is a view to a distant place:
Kitchen walls fall to reveal a gray sky,
an array of birds in flight through fog
—the crushed white of waves curling at feet.
There appears a woman in forested hair,
eyes of black pearl,
who touches the hewn face of a man
and palms that feel like bark.
She cringes at its blemishes
and something in her careens
against the walls of her heart.
She never wants to let go,
never wants to stop tracing
the scars above his eyebrows,
the tattoos on blackened skin,
while the lick of a tongue
stirs the night inside her.

The old woman looks at water and into
this vision shaped into a mouth
—the mouth of the sea that swallowed
her sailor-husband
so many sunlit windows ago.

from Notes of a Bald Cricket

1.
I sit alone, a bald cricket, in a bar on "poetry" night, face in a bottle,
singing the amber waves of beer. Poetry is the excuse,
as good as any. Be true to my art. But this is not what keeps
me here. It's the way tequila germinates inside like a knotted tree,
the way bodies darken into a sort of sunken beauty,
lights low and voices high, the way I can swim between these
back-lit walls. There is death to meet us, swollen hands
to wake us, a life that is falling into the gaps in the floor under our feet.
There are levels of delusions not even churches can attain.
Alchemists straddle bar stools, transformers and transformed,
awaiting my arrival into their webs of splintered stories
while manacled to curled ghosts called gin. I want to trace
the lies on women's skins, to vanish in their wine-drenched
eyes. I want to be flute and whisper, pubic hair and cumshot,
to warrant enough attention so they try to run me over in their cars.
I pause between lingering words, imagining their flight above me,
words to pull into my mouth, to drown into a shot glass,
words of infinite pain, a pain without words; words that claw
at the ceiling, that cough up blood, words that vomit
out of me in back alleys beside rat shit and wet cardboard;
words that slap me silly, that want to rifle through a man's wallet
and slip a hand beneath a woman's skirt; words that eat *tacos de pollo*,
with extra-hot *salsa*, that play muted trumpet into the reeking streets,
words to drown out the el train rumbling overhead, drowning out my
                                                                    words.
Crying can't speak. Tears only fall into empty palms. Tears & nights.
Night becomes the texture of memory, a humid breath glistening
perspiration on my forehead. Wandering from table to table,
my glass held unsteadily in my hand, I stave off hungers
even a double-champ cheeseburger with bacon cannot do.
Hungers for my friend's girlfriend, blue-eyed, dark-haired,
Polynesian-and-Irish, whose fingers I reach out for, whose hair

I want to shampoo, whose body I long to tread upon as if it were
autumn woods or a stretch of beach, with my toes deep into damp sand.
Every smile is a door, every glance a large bed to lay my head, a pillow
of eyelashes to soften the fall. Tequila, *ron*, blue whiskey for a blue
emotion. Mammary glands to memory glands. Each recalling a *déjà vu*
of startled intent. There are feels I always want to feel. There are voices
I would rip faded curtains to hear. There are faces to break
chrome-backed glass for, reflections of a liquid stare into millenniums
of stares. I'm dawdling on the edge of this sea in a glass, this last vestige
of my mother's fears, this grandfather poison that poisoned
my grandfather, this nectar of dried screams, this bruised cant,
this woman who presses her nipples to my cheek, whose chatter
cannot be climbed, whose kisses are stained lullabies, who tells me
I belong, although I cannot fit, who dares the fool's lament,
the call and response of night crawlers, the tones beneath my rambling,
who has become the last shriek of tequila dreaming,
whom I now grieve, ambling to the funeral tune of a child's cry
pulsing silent yet determined inside me.
O for beauty's fists to pommel this mask into itself,
for taste that is candy and not porcelain,
for wisps of saliva to wither on my hair and my chin,
for words to nuzzle and soak my tongue,
for language's naked prowlness to enter these shoes,
for a bald cricket's lyrical death on a dance floor.

5.
....when the wasted poems become dawn and are not gray-speckled haze,
when the upholding structures collapse from their perjuries,
when the money-system no longer determines worth
and purgatory is no longer your driveway
when the factory-spawn stops lactating 'burbs,
whose milk is dioxin, drying up earth's blood,
when all value is inside of you,
when the wasteland's raped-terrain bursts green,
when the creative heart is the only blossoming.

7. Wading through the lush of memory, through speechless seconds,
seeing myself on the backhand of past lives, crumbling emotions
surround me, as this obsessive and irresponsible poetry man beckons
to write. To tell truths. Oh such a liar. I'm a sleeveless
jacket in a closet of worn clothes; I'm the incision of scarring verbs
across the faces of all my loves. This Mexican who is a stranger in Mexico,
this pocho who hates milk with his coffee, juice with his vodka, who speaks
English with an East L.A. accent and Spanish with an East L.A. accent.
This Tarahumara's lost son, this graveled tongue, this ghost
beneath every ruin, rising like jaguar's breath in a tropical storm.
All sacrifices reside in me, all jagged chests, all virgin hosts,
with the wreckage of two massive oceans, all bloods commingling,
this Moor whose poetry stains the library walls, this armor-plated
mail-wearing, sword-thrusting, Andalusian who flew landward
through Iberian coasts and those of Cem-Anahuac.
I am Cortez's thigh, I am the African beard, I am the long course hair
of Chichimeca skulls. I am Xicano poet, a musician who can't play
music as a musician is a poet who works in another language.
There is a mixology of brews within me. I've tasted them all, still fermenting
as grass-high anxieties. I am rebel's pen, rebel's son,
father of revolution in verse. I am capitalism's angry Christ,
techno-Quetzalcoatl, toppling the temples
of modern thievery, of surplus value in word-art
—exploited, anointed, and perhaps double-jointed.
There's a brown Goddess in my eye, a Guadalupana for the broken red
earth. The sacred is too sacred for walled cathedrals,
for incensed and baroque martyrs in vested garbs, for pulpit schemers
and sweat lodge fakers and garbled spiritualists on the best-selling lists.
I am disciple and elder. I am rockero and hip hop bandit,
rapping Aztlanese in-between brick-lined texts.
What do I know? What blazing knowledge can I spear?
Who can burn with me and not get burned?
Violence used to be great solace, alcohol my faithful collaborator, scratching
dank words from stale corners. Now there are whole cities in my gardens,
Mexika drums pulsing from my temples. Saxophone riffs streaming
from the sky like a waterfall into the canyons of my body.

Walls carry my name, walls and their luminant fractures.
Walk with me then. Walk with me to the Maya. Walk with me along
headstones
of past loves, past plans, long-gone junctures. Walk with me through
the forest of collective remembering, shamed and honored by the trees.
I'm no immigrant. I belong because I belong. I'm no shaggy stranger.
I'm the holy villain, the outlawed saint,
the most Godless and therefore dearest to the mystery.
Where suicide is not solution. Where poems
No longer puncture the phantoms.
Where walking with me is to become brethren to rain
and night sweats and the betrayed.

this disjointed sneering
this lifting of cranial foam
this museum of oppressions
this waiting to be held, to be a musical note
this coursing through a rapture of voices
this clogged heart in the traffic of hearts

New Poems

My Name's Not Rodríguez

My name's not Rodríguez.
It is a sigh of climbing feet,
the lather of gold lust,
the slave masters' religion
with crippled hands gripping greed's tail.
My name's not Rodríguez.
It's an Indian mother's noiseless cry,
a warrior's saliva on arrow tip, a jaguar's claw,
a woman's enticing contours on volcanic rock.
My real name's the ash of memory from burned trees.
It's the three-year-old child wandering in the plain
and shot by U.S. Calvary in the Sand Creek massacre.
I'm a Geronimo's yell into the canyons of the old ones.
I'm the Comanche scout; the Raramuri shaman
in soiled bandanna running in the wretched rain.
I'm called Rodríguez and my tears leave rivers of salt.
I'm Rodríguez and my skin dries on the bones.
I'm Rodríguez and a diseased laughter enters the pores.
I'm Rodríguez and my father's insanity
blocks every passageway,
scorching the walls of every dwelling.
My name's not Rodríguez; it's a fiber in the wind,
it's what oceans have immersed,
it's what's graceful and sublime over the top of peaks,
what grows red in desert sands.
It's the crawling life, the watery breaths between ledges.
It's taut drum and peyote dance.
It's the brew from fermented heartaches.
Don't call me Rodríguez unless you mean peon and sod-carrier,
unless you mean slayer of truths and deep-sixer of hopes.
Unless you mean forget and then die.
My name's the black-hooded 9mm-wielding child in all our alleys.

I'm death row monk. The eight-year-old gum seller
in city bars and taco shops.
I'm unlicensed, uninsured, unregulated, and unforgiven.
I'm free and therefore hungry.
Call me Rodríguez and bleed in shame.
Call me Rodríguez and forget your own name.
Call me Rodríguez and see if I whisper in your ear,
mouth stained with bitter wine.

Coal-Seller in White Dress

In the central marketplace, San Salvador, El Salvador;
December 1993

She was a honey-skinned girl,
maybe fourteen,
in a white skirt laced at the hem
with hair in brushed brilliance.
She packaged black stones of coal
into plastic bags; there were coals
all around her,
on heaps near her smudged leg,
on top of a table—around the side.
Smaller children, faces
blackened with carbon dust,
yammered out prices
while standing next to a worn shed.
They sold packages for coal-fueled
stoves to heat the cold nights
of the tropical days.
Their lungs were coated with dust;
it collected on eyelashes and eyebrows
like a macabre makeup.
These children lived and breathed
coal, lived inside of coal.
They had their beauty blighted
or brightened
as the nuggets piled around them.
The fourteen-year-old
smiled at me like so much candy,
eyes of so much rain;
she glanced up and beneath
a pall of coal fog she muttered

a faint hello as I dissipated like a cloud,
filling the room with thankfulness
and excruciating sorrow.

The Cockroaches I Married

My cockroaches have been with me like forever:
Several generations of roach families
have graced my cupboards and book shelves
for around thirty years.
They are likely related to the critters
I encountered when I first married.
Although my wife and I eventually
broke up, these cockroaches continued to haunt
my socks drawer and toaster.
Over the years, regardless of where I lived,
I've carried these roaches in boxes,
magazines, clothes, and electrical appliances.
They nestled in the crumpled creases
and the darkest recesses.
(I trust it was them—the darn things do look alike.)
Besides, every landlord I knew claimed
no roaches existed in their places
until I showed up!
Over time, I've tried everything to get rid
of the damn pests:
Bug sprays,
cucumber slices laid out in various corners,
roach motels,
and Chinese anti-roach chalk.
But somehow a few managed to survive
and stow away in my possessions
until I arrived at my next abode.
If I paid attention, I could have given
these creatures their own names:
Le Roché,
Cuca Rocha,
or Lord Bugingham.
They may end up as life-long partners;

they have outlasted most of my wives,
cars and jobs.
But over the years, I've accumulated
some horror stories.
Like when my kids were babies,
I'd turn on the lights and watch
cockroaches scurry across their small faces.
And I recall opening cereal boxes
from where the creatures scrutinized me
through bent antennas and beady eyes.
Or drinking coffee with roach pieces floating on top.
Miserable spawn.
Disease carriers.
Blatta orientalis.
Despite this, we lived for a long time
in a kind of human-insect détente.
Whereas, I once took morbid pleasure
in crushing their hideous, brown-winged bodies,
I soon allowed them to meander by
without crashing down on them
with my fist.
One morning, though, the cold war
escalated to a fighting war:
My teenage son woke up the household
with blood yells down the hall.
As he held his head in a tortured expression,
he cried out about the pain.
I drove him to the hospital, where a doctor
—who looked like he had been through
much cockroach combat—took out
a tiny vacuum cleaner, stuck it gently
into my son's ear, and sucked up a particularly
gruesome mother.
That did it. I had reached my limits:
I brought in the heavy artillery.

An exterminator arrived with the latest
pest control technology,
including using enzymes that stopped
a roach's outer shell from growing:
They were crushed by their own bodies.
(What a way to go).
I know, in the end, they'll probably win.
But the fight, I tell you, the fight's the thing.
Nowadays, I may spot a lone roach warrior,
but I've carried out the equivalent
of chemical warfare and economic sanctions.
It's me or the roaches, man.
As far as I'm concerned,
this partnership is over. *Punto y zas.*

Mickey Mouse Pancakes

The sun sprayed voluminous rays on the backyard
    where I paced in a sleepless walk among autumn leaves;

Your six-year-old daughter was under covers on her
    bed; wide awake, she screamed in her room that

time we made love in yours. "I have to take care of her,"
    you said, and I responded, "yes, you should," but thought,

"what about me?" That summer, I mowed, trimmed and pruned
    the grass and bushes, prompting a neighbor to tell me

"you're good for her." Before I arrived, the dried-up
    yard was spotted with weeds and dirt, and nothing

flowered of any color. I transported truck
    loads of debris from the backyard to the city dump,

teeming with flies and seagulls; I patched the leaky roof
    and re-painted the house. When your daughter got sick

for days with chicken pox boils on her skin—she laid
    down on the floor rug and wailed—I took care of her

while you worked, all the time watching you learn to hate me.
    My own two kids visited on weekends, and you

seemed to close down, unable to cull forth a warm tone,
    to say, "maybe your kids are important, too."

I hated this feeling—that everything was up for
    negotiation and one's children were bargaining chips.

I hated this sense that I could never belong here.
    Regardless of how much I made this house into

a home, it would never be home for me. Sometime later,
    after we broke up in a tearful fit, arguing

over who did what, and what belonged to whom,
    after months of the most barren of nights, I asked

my children what they remembered about you.
    They recollected the way you made them Mickey Mouse

pancakes, with batter carefully placed on a heated pan,
    and how butter and syrup slid off the browned ears;

they recalled the stories you told and trips to the park.
    I couldn't remember any of this. What came

to mind was you leaving our bed, turning away
    from me, and your way of hurting by not responding;

how much I wanted you to just linger in my arms,
    to know that I cried without crying, and that losing

you was releasing a vital part of myself.
    My kids reminisced about pancakes, hide-and-seek

games and the constant bickering with your daughter.
    I only recalled your back to me once too often.

My Nature Is Hunger

*There were many Aztec feminine energies associated with earth and
fertility. The main deity was known as* Toci, *but she was also called*
Tonantzin, Teteo Innan, Coatlicue, Cihuacoatl, Itzpapalotl, *and*
Tlazolteotl. *She was the great conceiver, the principle behind
regeneration, birth and rebirth. She was also represented as the opposite
concepts of decay and death, the taker of life—from the earth, to the
earth. In one of her many manifestations, this power was known as*
Tlaltecuhtli, *a frog-like earth monster with many eyes and many mouths
at her joints. In this aspect, her nature was hunger, a devouring deity,
eater of hearts and of souls.*

Anyway, don't come close.
I'm not harmless. I'm the ground swallowing.
I'm grass of thorns, insatiable dirt,
with green claws of vines and shrubbery.
My moss-furred tongue pulls you into entrails of roots and seeds.
I'm gaping petals like slimy smiles,
taking you in, deeper and tighter,
filling me with a phallic spear of flesh.
My many mouths are many cervixes.
My corpse is a garden, covered in earth skin
with toes as mountains, a terrain of stone eyes
and watery grimaces. Enter here and die.
Leave and be born.
Every burrow, every crevice, every dank cave,
is an eternal vagina that sucks, shapes and also shuns.
Outside me burst new life. Inside, a smothering death.
Out of my severed body, the world has bloomed.
Man of woman. Woman of woman.
So come, and get folded
by these coral fingers,
into my arms made of forests,
nuzzled by the music of my breath.

My eyes open toward the sky, where man and woman
eclipse into god, and a priest, in someone else's skin,
opens you up to be taken by me
—fearful Mother, terrible Mother,
nurturer that caresses you,
and with a blink, shreds your flesh beneath moonless night.

Exiled in the Country of Reason

For African American revolutionary Nelson Peery
on the occasion of his 75th Birthday

You have known roads as Langston
remembers rivers, as water flows through the cracked
earth, as the rust and dust settles into a steel mill's lament.
You have known roads, hoboing then laying down bricks,
plumbing level the offices and homes of a brick-lined America.
Rain drenched, the roads stretch across the years.
Once you showed me the structures in New York City
that you mortared to life and I thought about how
you also laid down stones for paths of learning,
paths of struggle—how you built a road inside me.

And the roads stretch on.

For more than 25 years, I have sought your counsel.
In you, dwell the graveled voices of a fractured century,
In you, echo the cries of hod carriers, mud mixers, melters and smelters,
In you, the song of resistance never dies,
In you, the sunlight behind the dark clouds of racial injustice breaks
                                                            through,
In you, the callused palm heralding healing forms a firmer grip,
In you, the storms to quench the intractable fires of class warfare
                                                            forever rages.

For 75 years you exiled yourself into the country of reason.

Here is where I have found residence:
In the road-stretched lines of your face,
in the father-love of your embrace,
as a world crumbles around its own madness,
and dwindles behind its calculated indignities

and tortured logics.
Here next to you, where knowledge
is an exploding bullet, I found home.

You are my most enduring and endearing teacher.

So as you looked into my suicide eyes so long ago,
as you found the life breaking out of this deadened soul,
as you took in this young slave and madman,
whose only vision came through the rifled bore of a gun,
you showed me this is not the way things have to be.

I believed because you believed.

Since then my life has been broken in two:
Before Nelson and after Nelson.
Since then I have tried—and failed, oh so often—
to emulate your spirit, your ways of knowing,
your patience and poetry. I had no other way to go.
And our love is the love of the same thing,
the rule of the eyes, ideas, and visions
of this martyred truth: Things don't have to be this way.

Now I have discovered the courage within
my own courage, to trace the poetry you expressed
inside my own expression.
Everything you have learned, anyone can learn,
you always said. Slow down, think, study.
Don't die until you have something to live for.

You believe because I believe.

Twenty-five years ago, when we first met in a simple house
in the cauldron called Watts,
I handed myself over to revolution
and have bled blossoms ever since.

I gave myself over to the brick-walled imaginations
that dared to dream a different dream.
For this I thank you, Nelson,
from where the tattered flag unfurls

and the road stretches on.

Passersby

Be passersby.

—Jesus of Nazareth to his disciples,
from the Gospel of Thomas.

You who walk this way, make this way,
the chance encounterer, the pacer of minute
steps, the one going no place and therefore every
place. Be a path maker who treads the ground
of no ground, where walking is life and this life
is its own meaning. Be a wanderer, not bound to these
graveled byways, or the four walls of family prisons
or the rule of law that hides great lawlessness.
Be the one who observes, listens and honors
all water and all breathing. Be as a migrant
and therefore a moment, as if not really there,
and yet always belonging.
Come into being as you walk past, an eternal
pedestrian, where the world is a bridge,
never a home. Tell the truth, a fleeting thing,
and be the truth, a fleeting person.
Knowing that time is a superb illusion
that quantum facts are also quantum lies,
that every knowledge is also no knowledge,
and that when you proceed, you fill the empty
space between us, as the one who truly understands,
who truly loves,
and then is gone.

Listening to Return To Forever's "Romantic Warrior" with Susana in an Empty Room of my Recently Rented Echo Park Apartment

Her eyes closed, lashes spread like spider's legs,
her hands beneath her head like pillows.
The soft down of hair on her arms
glistened with the light from the windows without curtains.
Her legs lay on their side, hips like a fertile hill,
wrapped in a work suit, nylons rubbed thigh to thigh.
My eyes swam over swirl of body
while the music unfurled around us;
it pulled me to that face, a pulse at her temple.
Each instrument a conversation:
Cello bass moan,
guitar fury,
and piano keys playing like children in a park.
Every phrase and notation,
reviving,
spinning,
calculating
the spiral of emotions
churning the sea of blood within me.

Mother by the Lake

To Chicago

1.

I face a procession of limbs,
Songs of eyes and things,
Seeing myself in what is less in others,
Succumbing to curbsides and flailing pigeons,
Dying to the graystone facades,
To downtown's naked topography.
Someone's dreamed this and therefore dreamed me.
I face my demise in the water fountains
Where the homeless nest, where words are crutches
On weathered pages. Promenade with these words as I do,
Pressing my way through dankness,
Blinded by scattered sentences and meaningless grunts.
I'm nailed to the sidewalk by gazes,
Stopped by accusations in pursed lips,
Defying death by strolling.
Glass, gum spots, winged newspapers,
Cracked pens, bites of food, unbitten.
Save me, or get out of the way.

2.

Mother, I can't cry through ego.
I can't find the sensual through plastic covers.
I'm only what I've coughed up.
I'm only the lamp without the light.
I'm only the sun's stretching fingers
Pulling us up when standing.
We'd be slithering if not for this.
O Mother, I crawled on your belly
And you've held me ever since.
You the ground; Father the sky.

I'm going toward him even as you draw me
Toward your breasts. The sky can wait.
I'm nudging myself a space between dumpsters
And withered cardboard.
Mother, you've nestled me to these waters
And I can't swim.

3.

Soot-stained lyrics fill the crevices between brick.
El train brakes on metal rails make a sonata for junk dogs:
A blues that never stops.
Stray cats and black-eyed rats roam the unfenced yards.
I've fallen into cobblestone love affairs.
I've stared at bridges and viaducts and potholes
And wondered what planet I was in.
Murder here is the source spring of new life.
A gun is a character in the drama between screams.
Bullets make for great lullabies.
Market cart alley shoppers take all the best deals.
If heartache were a city it would be Chicago.
If suicide had eyes, it would be the lonely gaze
Of skyline at the edge of lake.

Suicide Sweet

1. Tlayollo : Heart of Earth

The object of Nights is simple: You must retrieve five dreams,
then defeat a boss.
        —From instructions to a Japanese-made video game.

Stones.
Passive hands on moon-starved shores
The way of letting go : won't let go
Water culls the starved rocks to their suns
Songs then tears then the gray cliff
The flight of wingless death
O home is there : monotony
Let flesh direct its own shadow
If the flowers are blue : the birds are squatting sores
O Poets : distracted by the laughter of trees

How to abandon our skins
To essential coffee
To arterial germ in the lake of our logics
Lori Jackson haunts these lines
El Gallo roams the running board of this poem
There's Jimi Hendrix : electricland tour buses
Have their engines running : can't be late
(don't tell me overdoses are not suicides)
Kurt Cobain growls : heroin then a shotgun blast
Phyllis Hyman is a diva forever

I want to be there : catatonic

I'm high and my feet demand ground
My sorrows ricochet between limbs and bark

We all participate in the end
Should I leap : should I creep
The choices have their own eyes
Should I pray : should I make the bed
Body dances away but not the betrayals

Dying this way is not a U-turn
Nobody jumps into the dark behind you
I leave the footprints of my spirit on the carpet
Don't wash it out : don't let it stain
I sense the uselessness of this dread
What does it matter? I wish it would stop
If the air wasn't so inviting
I would step back into the safety of walls
I would stagger on the toes
Of my failed words

The five dreams elude me

2. Itlatol Temictli : The Dream of a Word

And, O friends, hear the dream of a word: Each spring gives us
life, the golden ear of corn refreshes us, the tender ear of corn
becomes a necklace for us. We know that the hearts of our
friends are true!

Fingers.
The pressures over eyebrow : the sweet terrain
Momentary glances know : remember those lips
What awakens in me flows like a waterfall
So for a poem to be born
Many things must die
O my heart aches for this
I need poems to catch me : rudimentary

The Indian girl writes a poem
Then jumps into a jagged cloud
There is no Indian word for suicide

A gay man bleeds his poems
On a bathroom tile floor
It matters what people think
You say it doesn't? Oh, really?
Funny?? You ?? Should ?? Ask???
The matter that is not chemical composition
That is not helixes and amniotic fluid
Is what matters : synchronicity
What is not touched is faked
What is not faked must be faced
What is not faced is forgotten
So what's final is not formidable

If words could dream
They'd be this wild

3. Zitlalxochitl : The Star That Becomes A Flower

> What is poetry which does not save
> —Czeslaw Milosz

Nights.
All first years are bathed in silence
When we were ourselves : we never died to wind
When we grew our own laws : the laws took care of us
The laws that are alien are always against us
We do not walk the same way on this earth
Some have sturdy legs
Others have been maimed
The dialectic of life is to rebalance
Jesus says the last will be first : reciprocity

A mouth full of weeds will bear curses

Learn to die inside every life
And behold the life in every death
Be still : the rhythms of the world fall like rain
In the soil of your traumas : geraniums
If you've known many men : you've known a woman

Lingering and lingering
Once you've tried the jump
You always keep jumping
Remember : learn to die inside your life
Jump again and again: be free on the other side

Every flower has star power
Every bursting sun is the breath of babies
Just say : we're all responsible
Blame yourself for the worse things
Then know you've made a better world

Die and live : we need more poems

Sometimes a Man Comes

Sometimes a man comes whose walk is the habit of winds,
Who negates the ambush of alcohol & drugs
And this cruelty of boulevards called "the life."
Sometimes a man like this becomes the schooled body
Of the schooled soul, whose healing is an utterance,
Who menaces with light, whose passion is a
Mathematical caring, whose wisdom is a laughing spear,
And whose scars are the secret language of home.

Sometimes a man comes who holds unfathomable sorrows in his eyes
And sacrifices what no one else will dare for the law of eagles.
Sometimes we are awakened petals because of such a man,
                                    such a woman,
Such a human being, architects of tender tasks.
This man is our blessing way, our stilled blood, singing bones,
Graveyard tears, cracked shells, secret errors, terrible triumphs, and
                                    wild moons.

Sometimes a man comes who turns an enemy into a friend,
Who reaches out to fallen poets in their shadowed need
And sweeps the ashes of our lives through the doorways
Of inebriated battle. Sometimes, but not always, we are victory's legs,
Water's blue & endless deserts because of such a man,
Such a woman, such a human being. In their glow, we become
Auras and flames, re-imagined in their embrace,
Ignited by their words, leaning always toward their last breath
While standing unsteadily on a mountain's ledge leering at clouds.

Time and Nature

For Maria Estela

Time knows mother's tears as a son knows
When he awakens and finds his mother has cried
Them and he never listened. My mother is now
Old, fraught with cancerous cells, held together by steel
Bars from the many times she has fallen and busted up bones.
She is feeble but strong. Her spirit dense in the space
Of creaky woman body she inhabits. In my visits, she
Sits next to me, holding my hand, happy
To know I'm there. I'm sad. For thirty years
We seldom talked. For years before that we were at war.
I was the gang son, the drug user, the runaway,
The "incorrigible"—a crime because a mother's
Beatings could no longer tame me. And I'm unsure
Sitting there—I wasn't such a good son,
She wasn't such a good mother. So many years
And pains between us. But what else can we do?
A friend says I should tell her what I feel,
About how much her curses still ring in my ears,
How her defense of a soul-dead and heart-sick father
Coiled a rage inside of me, how
When I needed protection, she turned the other way.
Yet what good does tearing down a wall do
When time and nature have already battered it to rubble?
It's simple to be next to her, in the quiet, by her breathing
And grasping her hand like a child. Simple and right.
No need to raise the residue of what's dead when our touching
Names what's alive. I've had my say. It's enough that my mother
Smiles when I smile. That she has become a gentle
And stable soul in her evening of life. It's enough
That I've returned home—and that I still dream the big dreams.

It's enough that my mother, who railed hard against them for so long,
Says it's fine, so good, to have such dreams.
Loving my mother, something I always did, now
Fits like melodious rain and the falling of leaves.
I just had to let family bring us back.
And that's enough until I can't see her anymore
And love becomes the air between the dead and the living,
Between earth and cloud,
Between our last yelling living room encounter
And a sigh falling gently into the flowerbed.

Loving What You Leave

The alley behind our Logan Square house brimmed with old books,
Shelves, toys, kitchen utensils, worn tools, and tired clothes.
Leaving Chicago meant parting from the corpses of old styles,
Loves, musics, moments, and wet encounters.
It wasn't just things we left lying there—it was what we
Couldn't hold except between arguments.
Our young sons didn't want to go—what do parents
Have to do for their kids when uncertainty
Fails the pleadings? But they would learn to love LA,
Home where their mother and I were raised, learn to love
What's not to love because what's to love
Is worth loving.
There was family in LA—tons of cousins, many aunts
And uncles, and their one grandmother who still
Graced this ground with her presence.
If not they were going to have to live
With what they didn't love.
Moving is a major cause of suicides or breakups.
I knew this—I had moved so often, my possessions
Often in unopened boxes.
A street dude from the 'hood named Cholo
Helped us pack the moving truck;
He knew what he was doing—tattooed
Body glistening in the sun, putting everything
In the truck, neat and compact.
But the truck took off the next morning
Without the required bulkhead.
When it arrived in LA, much of our things had been crushed
In the 2,000 miles or so it took to get there.
We didn't break up, commit suicide or kill anybody
—oh, but we wanted to.

Ritchie Valens Doesn't Sing Here Anymore

Pacoima is a native word for running waters.
It is also one of those dreaded, poor barrios of LA
Rife with gangs, including Pacas, the original
Varrio here with its legacy on walls, the housing
Projects and blurred tattoos.
When we first came here, I stayed in the same house
My wife grew up in. But one house?
This was something I couldn't understand
Having lived in a dozen homes before I turned 18.
One morning I walked around these streets to gather in
its smells, feels, noises, and sights...the neighbors.
A black woman walked onto her porch and told me
"We ain't going to carry you people anymore!"
A drunken white guy demanded I go back to where I came
From. Five *vatos* rushed out of an alley;
One carried a machete in his hand.
They ran past me, hardly noticing I was there, and
Kept pace toward their intended victims on another
Block. At Ritchie Valens Recreational Center, I stopped
To admire the mural of Pacoima's favorite son,
Creator of a sound in rock that actually came from
Veracruz, Mexico (where descendents of Olmec Indians,
Africans, and Spanish made a *mole* of culture). He died too young,
At 17 from a plane crash in a snowy field in Ohio. Buddy Holly
And Big Bopper also earned Angel wings that night.
Pacoima has had hard times ever since.
Van Nuys Boulevard looks more like a busy street in
Tijuana. And the houses get more crowded and dirtier with each year.
I like Pacoima. It's funky. Roosters can't tell time. And
Rancheras and *cumbias* play all night on weekend *barbacoas*.
But then innocent nine-year-old girls get shot in drivebys.

And one Pacoima man was convicted of killing
Two of his 13 children, which he had from two sisters,
And forcing the older kids to bury them along a desert road.
One thing is certain—there may be a lot of singing
Going on, but Ritchie Valens doesn't sing here anymore.

Mexika Science

In a roll of iguanas sunning on a dirt road
Is the answer to all the mysteries of the world.
In the dewdrops that are feed for the appetites
Of the gods, what grows also dies.
Duality is the language of genetic memory
—the supreme generating principle of the universe.
All knowledge is contained in one thought
And expressed in millions.
When the Spanish found the 60,000 amate-paper
Books in the cubby holes of Mexika temples,
It was the conquerors who were frightened, not the Natives.
The science and spirituality fused had the highest order
—and it was destroyed, as were the temples, the goddesses,
The laws, the gardens, the menageries, the elder
System, and the poems. Only fear could exact such brutality.
Everything destroyed so nothing could challenge the barbarians
Who called themselves the civilized, who called themselves
The children of God, who in the falsehoods of their truth,
Would rather that a whole people be eliminated
Than to face the wealth of aligned thought
To reality to nature to the cosmos and to deep earth past.

The Gold Beneath Our Feet

The Basilica in Rome, a sunny day, with thousands
Waiting to enter the massive doors of church
And center. I came, too, having been raised in its
Spherical domain, but now long without the
Stone walls to contain me. I arrived with daughter
And friend, not to pay homage, but to see,
To feel, to know why, again, I raged for justice
Inside a gilded castle. The only justice with eyes.
The floors were inlaid with gold, gold statues
Loomed over us, brass candle holders
At every altar. Polished wood confessional booths
Pushed up against thousand-year-old walls
Where penitents and priests commune in common
With sin. Many prayed, whispering, solemn, at awe.
I seethed—blood like magma vomits of earth,
Dense dark of past irreconciled.
It was a tomb for me, for bitter-bone history that sculptured
My bones. I did not feel the sacred, but the dead,
The screams, the eyeless songs,
The people sacrificed for the gold that now
Emblazoned this coffin, watered by tears of lead,
Greeted by guttural laughs,
Lined with charred flesh and charred poems.

Banned

Books more fearsome than monsoons;
Thunder clouds of words & earthquakes.

Splintered spines. Words to worry.
Spitting truths to public seashores,

Beached truths like whales out of water.
Afraid to drown in these truths, better

To breathe freely in the lies—the nature of man.
Words to marry. Love without truth.

Words to cut swaths of concrete
Roads through forested mountains.

Banned. Burned. Tossed. Books
To awaken the sleeping woman,

The dried-heart man. Barter
The bitter brine of bogus bigotry.

We've been banned, purgatory
—minds, stillborn but vital.

Banned. Oh, intimate collusion
Between page and purpose.

Fat

We're all fat in America, even the anorexics,
Fat with fat lies and fat fears and fat schemes.

I've been fat for fifteen years—and exercise,
Pills, diets, doctors, stress, and Trader Joe's

Food can't change that. This fat covers
Sorrows, past indiscretions, slow death,

Addictions and shunned silences that
Shaped me. Fat. Not cool. But forever?

Fat is cruelty leveled against the cruel.
Glutton tastes demand more for less.

Beer yeast fat. Fat of trigger hand
And jail cell eyes. Fat of ego and thinness

Of talent. Fat in cheeks, hands,
Buttocks and a magnificent belly.

Fat around the heart. Traffic of blood
Engorged. They say it's lack of willpower

That makes us fat. Yes, brain folds
Can overcome skin folds. Will power—

Why didn't I think of this before? Think
My way out of being fat...imagine that!

No matter, we're all fat in America.
Even thin models are full of themselves.

The Chuskas—Navajo Land 1998

Ring of rainbow stones surround these sage stone people.
Age and rust amount to the same thing.

The Diné say they're protected by the Four
Sacred mountains that embrace these

Fruitless soils. To be so close to the land you're
Enslaved by—they know true religion.

In the sand painting chants and prayer
Meeting smoke inside teepees or *hogans*

They're free because they're not. The
Land, the brush, the dirt and mesas

Say, "you're home. Don't ever leave again."
My bones are made of the same iron/uranium/copper

Faces on these stones. Peabody Co. tears the
Heart out of each mountain from the inside.

They know rape. Cultural make-up. Rape
Is the great metaphor and reality. Tear my

Heart out then. What you sacrifice you
Also give to me. Rust and root in the Chuskas.

Rez Dogs

The Navajo boy says to us men standing outside
The government housing on the rez. "You like
My haircut?"—"sure," "looks cool," "yeah."
"Fuck you...what do I care what you think"
Nothing to do on the rez but fuck with people.
A Skinwalker brushes up against you and you
Better be in good thoughts. Or those thoughts
Will forever be your thoughts. Who cares
What you think? A Skinwalker does.
Rez dogs wheeze by, bones through the skin,
Showing teeth but too sick to bark. One rez
Dog was tied to a pole to guard chickens.
Since it was a puppy, it never knew anything
But that chain and pole—rain, shine or dark—
barking like mad to keep coyotes away.
Its brother, born at the same time,
Lived in the house. It ate good food
And had plenty of petting hands and comfort.
Fate knows what it wants. Skinwalkers do, too.
That's why you don't take them lightly
Or turn away from what you can't see.
Remember it can see you. Keep your inner
Eyes open. They see further on the rez,
Further down the road with miles and miles
Of suspension-destroying bumps & sinkholes,
Toward what Fate throws at you, and you
Can't turn away fast enough to avoid.

Untitled

An abandoned adobe hut, crumbled
Walls, gaps in roof, glassless window openings,
Dirt floor with wine bottles, aerosol
Spray cans and soiled newspapers
Pushed up against the corners.
My Navajo friend called it "The
Battered Husband Shelter."

¡Si, Se Puede! Yes, We Can!

For the Los Angeles Janitor's Strike, April 2000

Beneath steel and concrete,
Beneath night's wandering shadow,
Come the eyes, voices and arms—elbows and knees—
That make buildings shine, magnifying the sun into all our faces.
The nameless, the scorned, the ignored—yet
They are the humanity that makes human things work.

Mothers and children, fathers and uncles, family and family—
They come to make this city dance, the rhythm of what's just,
What is secure—the dance of strike and protest,
                              demand and dignity.
They toil inside these glass temples—they clean them—
The truly human who now step into the streets,
                              into our tomorrows,
And declare: *¡Basta!* Enough! What we clean, we also make
sacred.

Chuparosa (Hummingbird)

My wife Trini loves *chuparosas*.
One often comes to her, praise in its wings,
Sister to sister, as Trini walks up to the red
Bloom in the bushes and it hovers
In silent recognition of bird
And this flower called woman.

A *chuparosa* once got caught below the window awning.
It moved end to end, fear in its flutter,
As I watched it try to escape.
Unable to do anything, I directed its path
With my eyes. For a moment, it was Trini held,
In the paralyzing mud/mode she often falls into.
I knew the bird would find a way out
As Trini always does, drawing on her
Intensity of decency that scares
Most people whose decency
Is mostly a burden below thin veil.

In the *chuparosa*'s work—nectar seeker
And midwife to all blossoms—
I see Trini. In another life, they
Are mother and daughter,
Feed to all color and sweet nature.
There's dance and grace
In their motion, suspended around
The ugly hard things
Like gnarled tree—or me—
Struggling with mountains to persist.

Existence

There's a tribe in South America
That desires to die off—they won't eat,
Hunt or gather fruit. Die off because
They say they dreamed
The White Man's coming
And if they die, so will that dream.

Nightfall: Poems to Ponder in War and Uncertainty

When prisons become the fastest growth industry
Our minds and hearts become the imprisoned

When the past of blood and conquest is denied
The land gives back this blood in torrents

When war is the only imagination of the people
The people's imagination becomes an insurrection

When we sacrifice lives, including our children's
Evil becomes as common as breathing

When truth scares us to apathy
Our only truths come from the most fantastic lies

When enemies are whoever our leaders say they are
We won't know an enemy from a rainbow

When power and wealth drives social policy
All policies are subject to poetic death

When my son asks, do I have to go to war?
A father's duty is to war against war first

When people say peace is the absence of conflict
They have no idea what they're talking about

When war forces us to die outside of ourselves,
We have to learn to live from inside our bones.

***

I read the newspapers today
and the climate reports again proclaimed
perpetual nightfall.
I read the newspapers and saw that things
are worse for our children then they were for us.
I turned on the TV and found the darkening
pulling us along fast-moving swollen rivers,
where we grasp at unstable stones and loose branches
only to be swept away into the shadows
next to "welcome" doormats and canary cages.

***

Our leaders have called in the troops
with one or two syllable declarations.
Imagination is a casualty of this war
as are poetic language and moral consistency.
Despite millions taking to the streets against war
we go to war anyway because, hey, we got the weapons.
This is a democracy that doesn't care that people care.
This is a country that fights evil with guns
although this is evil's playground,
that opposes affirmative action in colleges
but pushes affirmative action in the military,
that has no vision, although there's plenty to see,
that has no dreams, although there's plenty of sleeping,
that denies reality, although there's plenty
of reality shows.

***

Walk with the young, America,
be young, again, America,
be among the defiant and awake,
solid in their dreams.
Be the revolution in the marrow
where passions, ideals, fervors,
purposes and courage
are not just something
people had in history books,
but what we have to possess everyday,
anytime repression, injustice,
fear and greed
gather like night riders
about the gallop
through our living rooms.

***

Where will your fingers take you when you can no longer
trace the lines on your mother's face? When will a child's
cry stop being the breath of morning? As war becomes
the milk in our cereal, the rain on our sill, the constant
rattle beneath our car's hood—so much a part of everything—
we lose the conception of life without war.

we lose what it is to be alive without killing.

***

I see the lost youth of America
finding their way
with plenty to fight for, not just against.
Thousands marching across the land,
walking out of schools, putting up signs,

145

and talking the ears off their friends.
Rigorous, animated and brave
instead of sad and silent down the hallways.

***

Education cannot be confined to fenced buildings.
It is in the heart, at home, in the parks, in the mall.
Schools don't teach, you say?
Then choose to learn anyway.
Fight for the schools, but never stop accepting
that with caring, with community,
education is everywhere.

***

The parents of the dead Iraqi War soldier
have pictures of their daughter on a mantel
with photos of childhood school faces
and softball teams next to certificates and trophies.
These are monuments to their quiet complicity,
their confused collaboration
in her sacrifice—something they must never
acknowledge even as their tragic mistake
haunts their sullen walk in every room of the house.

The Wanton Life

For my son Ramiro,
sentenced to 28 years in the Illinois Department of Corrections

The long fingers of a wanton life,
from the ends of a twisted highway,
pull at us with the perfume of the streets
and its myriad romances,
all intoxicating, gripping at our skins;
as blasts of late-night shoot-outs,
the taste of a woman's wet neck in a dark alley,
and the explosion of liquor bottles
against a cinder-block wall
free us from the normal world,
while chaining us to the warped cement walks
of our diminished existence.

I run with you inside of me
entering layers of darkness,
into the swaddling of night,
with accelerating thoughts,
in the velocity of the city's demands,
constantly moving, but inside standing still,
searching for words to cut through the drivel,
the screams around my ears,
the pain of neglect and addictions,
running with your voice in my throat,
you, calling out my name,
searching for father while I searched for mine,
on your earth of many souls,
craving the moon,
the lunacy and warmth
of these rocks covered in mud.

I dreamt I had a son.
His name was Ramiro.
He was a beautiful boy.
He loved his father.
He laughed and played and smiled.
I dreamt such a great boy.
I woke up.
And the nightmare of the reality told me,
I should be there.

The outlaw life, idealized, symbolized,
even kids who've never truly lived are "killas;"
it's in the rhymes, in the bass, in the rhythms
from inside bouncing cars or yawning windowpanes.
Tattoos on faces—they're saying, you can't change this;
you can't change me.
Permanent pathology.
But that's only the body.
Inside, somewhere, there's a different song
Who will listen to that song?
Who will know these cries because they've languished here, too.
The truth is we're all broken.

What regrets and longings must we bear?
What clutch of inner fears forces our hand?
What frenzy knocks on our door
and then when we open it,
darkness is swept in?
Do we need more laws but less humanity?
More punishment and less redemption?
As Common asks, "High expectations but low patience?"
Fear drives policy and then drives us from being human.
It's time to understand, go open-eyed into ourselves,
into our deepest fears, among our underground youth,

into the futureless future, and then rise up.
The time of sleeping is over.

The falling is so forceful,
a gravity of soul to the bottom.
The motion downward takes in reams of unwritten poetry,
paintings with no canvases,
notes without melodies.
As a young man, I wanted somebody to stop me,
to stop me from crumpling into the death surrounding me,
the death that gives one life.
I didn't seem to be able.
Sometimes prison can work this way
—most of the time it keeps you falling, further, deeper.
The key to life is to have the words,
the images and the songs as the barriers to all the great falls.

Collapse into yourself;
fold into the pages of your journals,
into the chords in your head,
into what your heart sees.
Every other choice has death in it,
so choosing your death seems empowering.
Art is about creativity,
new breath, new birth.
The only empowering course that echoes,
that ripples, that takes on new shapes as it goes outward.
Not down—lateral to the rest of us.
It took me a while, but I learned to fall sideways.

LUIS J. RODRÍGUEZ—of Mexika-Raramuri descent—is founder-director of Tía Chucha Press and a cofounder of Tía Chucha's Cafe Cultural and its not-for-profit arm, Tía Chucha's Centro Cultural—a bookstore, café, art gallery, performance space, workshop space, and computer center in Sylmar, CA. He's also cofounder and editor of the Xicano online magazine, *Xispas.com.*

Luis was a leading figure in the East Los Angeles art and poetry scene of the early 1980s, emanating from Self-Help Graphic Arts Center's Barrio Writers Workshops and Echo Park's Galeria Ocaso; he also published and edited *XismeArte* magazine.

In 1988, three years after moving to Chicago, he became active in that city's vibrant poetry movement, including poetry slams that have now become an international phenomena. He was a cofounder/board member of Chicago's Guild Complex, a leading literary and arts presentation organization; an organizer for the Chicago Poetry Festival; and he has facilitated poetry workshops and readings in prisons, homeless shelters, juvenile facilities, public and private schools, community centers, migrant camps, universities, and bookstores for around 30 years.

After publishing three award-winning poetry books, Rodríguez released his first CD of music and poetry with Dos Manos Records in 2002 titled "My Name's Not Rodríguez." He presently resides in San Fernando, CA.

CURBSTONE PRESS, INC.

is a non-profit publishing house dedicated to literature that reflects a commitment to social change, with an emphasis on contemporary writing from Latino, Latin American and Vietnamese cultures. Curbstone presents writers who give voice to the unheard in a language that goes beyond denunciation to celebrate, honor and teach. Curbstone builds bridges between its writers and the public – from inner-city to rural areas, colleges to community centers, children to adults. Curbstone seeks out the highest aesthetic expression of the dedication to human rights and intercultural understanding: poetry, testimonies, novels, stories, and children's books.

This mission requires more than just producing books. It requires ensuring that as many people as possible learn about these books and read them. To achieve this, a large portion of Curbstone's schedule is dedicated to arranging tours and programs for its authors, working with public school and university teachers to enrich curricula, reaching out to underserved audiences by donating books and conducting readings and community programs, and promoting discussion in the media. It is only through these combined efforts that literature can truly make a difference.

Curbstone Press, like all non-profit presses, depends on the support of individuals, foundations, and government agencies to bring you, the reader, works of literary merit and social significance which might not find a place in profit-driven publishing channels, and to bring the authors and their books into communities across the country. Our sincere thanks to the many individuals, foundations, and government agencies who have recently supported this endeavor: Community Foundation of Northeast Connecticut, Connecticut Commission on Culture & Tourism, Connecticut Humanities Council, Greater Hartford Arts Council, Hartford Courant Foundation, Lannan Foundation, National Endowment for the Arts, and the United Way of the Capital Area.

Please help to support Curbstone's efforts to present the diverse voices and views that make our culture richer. Tax-deductible donations can be made by check or credit card to:
Curbstone Press, 321 Jackson Street, Willimantic, CT 06226
phone: (860) 423-5110   fax: (860) 423-9242
www.curbstone.org

IF YOU WOULD LIKE TO BE A MAJOR SPONSOR OF A
CURBSTONE BOOK, PLEASE CONTACT US.